MV AGUSTA AMERICA

Jeff Clew

CONTENTS

Foulis

Haynes

Further titles in this series will be published at
regular intervals. For information on new titles
please contact your bookseller or write to the
publisher

ISBN 0 85429 334 5

A FOULIS Motorcycling Book

First published 1983

Published by:
Haynes Publishing Group
Sparkford, Yeovil,
Somerset BA22 7JJ

Distributed in USA by:
Haynes Publications Inc.
861 Lawrence Drive, Newbury
Park, California 91320 USA

Editor: Rod Grainger
Dust jacket design: Rowland Smith
Page Layout: Madaleine Bolton
Colour photography: Andrew Morland
Road tests: Courtesy of *Motorcycle
Sport* and *Cycle*
Printed in England by: J.H.Haynes &
Co. Ltd

FOREWORD

Fittingly described as the Lamborghini of the motorcycling world, the road-going 750cc MV fours brought a touch of the exotic to those who really know and enjoy motorcycling to the full. The first of the modern in-line fours, there can be little doubt that the ancestors of the America inspired Japanese thinking and led to the emergence of the Honda fours, culminating in the debut of the CB750 during 1969. Destined to become the first mass-produced 'Superbike', over 61,000 CB750s were sold in the USA alone during the first three years of manufacture. But therein lay the difference between the Japanese four and its Italian counterpart. With an incredible number of World Championship successes to its credit, the MV represented the very epitome of Italian motorcycle engineering at its best. Although made in only comparatively small numbers, and over a brief span of time too, the road-going versions of the Grand Prix racers attracted the more discerning purchaser, to whom price was only a secondary consideration. There was something very special about owning an MV four, especially the 750cc America. Just to look at it was sufficient to conjure up visions of those epic race battles between Surtees and McIntyre or Agostini and Hailwood. An MV parked by the roadside could be guaranteed to draw a crowd anywhere, as indeed still happens today.

Sadly, I have never owned one of these fabulous machines — but we can all dream and even writing about them gives me untold pleasure. In the days when I raced, there would sometimes be an MV in the paddock at the big international meetings and later, when I was BEMSEE Travelling Marshal, I was with them on the starting grid. At that time I regarded myself as being very privileged, for it seemed inconceivable that over-the-counter road-going versions would ever be available. But it happened for just a few years until MV decided to concentrate on their main business of making helicopters. The MV four came and went, leaving a gap at the top end of the market that has never been filled. A tribute to the America is therefore long overdue, which is a situation I hope I can in some way rectify within the pages of this book.

It would be true to say that much of this book could have not been written without the enthusiastic help of Dave Kay, Secretary of the MV Agusta Owners Club. I was fortunate to come across Dave at the 1982 Classic Bike Show and once he knew of my intention to write this book, he offered me every possible assistance. Dave is a good and very knowledgeable mechanic, whose machines feature in the photographic section. I would like to ensure that his help in checking the manuscript and suggesting where improvements and/or corrections should be made does not pass unnoticed either.

Owner interviews, an important section of this book, were kindly provided by Dave and four other MV Agusta Owners Club members, Mark Wellings, Bill Hicks, Bill Johnson and Peter Eacott. The photographs were taken by Andrew Morland, using the four machines made available by Dave Kay. The National Motor Museum supplied the racing photographs from their photographic library archives and my good friend Cyril Ayton made up the balance of photographs from material held by *Motorcycle Sport*, of which he is Editor.

Jeff Clew

HISTORY

Many will be surprised to learn that the early origins of the MV four stem from the Gilera four, or 'Rondine' as it was known originally. This comes about because Ing. Pietro Remor laid out the original design of the four-cylinder engine and took much expertise with him when he left Gilera to join MV in 1947. The company takes its name from the village in which the factory is located – Verghera, Agusta being the name of the wealthy and titled family that controls the company and has run the motorcycling side more as a hobby than a serious commercial enterprise. The 'M', of course, if for *Meccanica*.

It was during April 1950 that advance details of a new four-cylinder design were released to the Press, and when the first photographs were released a month later it could be seen that there was a strong family resemblance between the MV and Gilera racing designs. But the MV design differed in at least two major respects, both of which related to the suspension. The front forks were of the blade girder type and the rear swinging arm arrangement of the parallel ruler type with movement controlled by Hartford-type friction dampers. Both the front and the rear suspension used torsion bars, the friction dampers at

the rear being fitted to prevent a 'pogo stick' effect on uneven surfaces. As may be expected from such an unorthodox set-up, the handling at high speeds proved to be anything but good and the suspension system became the subject of many modifications.

The four-cylinder engine was set across the duplex frame, which had a single top tube and box-section rear members. It sloped slightly forward and had the gearbox built in-unit. With bore and stroke measurements of 54 x 54mm, the engine was of the dohc type, in which the camshafts were driven by a train of helical gears. The sparking plugs were centrally disposed and on the initial design, only two carburetters were fitted. The press photographs showed straight-through exhaust pipes, which terminated by the front of the rear wheel, but when the machine was raced, megaphones were added. It was not long before each cylinder had its own carburetter rather than sharing with its neighbour.

Brakes were of the drum type, both being of large diameter. The fuel tank had built-in knee recesses and there was a pad on top of the tank to protect the rider's chin when he was in the 'flat out' riding position. The dry weight was alleged to be 290lbs and it was claimed the engine would produce about 50bhp at 10,000rpm. The four-speed gearbox, with cross-over final drive permitted a maximum speed of fractionally under 130mph under optimum conditions.

Over the next three years many changes in specification were made to try and improve the handling, but it was not until Les Graham was persuaded to leave the AJS racing team and join MV that significant improvements were made. Les was a superb rider who possessed that rare ability of being able to translate problems encountered under racing conditions into practical solutions, and it was a bitter blow when he

lost his life on Bray Hill during the 1953 Senior TT. Already the big MV had begun to show its paces, Les having taken 2nd place in the 1952 Senior TT and set the record lap in the Ulster Grand Prix later that same year.

Not unexpectedly, the MV team was demoralised by this setback, despite the fact that Bill Lomas, Cecil Sandford and Dickie Dale were given works rides in the 1954 Junior and Senior TT races. Deperately needing another really topline rider, the MV management succeeded in persuading Ray Amm to join them after Norton Motors had decided to withdraw from the World Championship hunt. But once again their luck ran out. Early in 1955, his first season with MV, Ray came off at Imola and was killed instantly when he struck an iron post. The only win recorded that year was in the Italian Grand Prix, when Masetti brought his 500 four into first place – a popular win on home territory. Fortunately, the smaller capacity twins gave a better account of themselves, MV taking the 250cc and 125cc World titles at the end of the season.

A full-page announcement in the December 1st, 1955, issue of *Motor Cycling* brought the welcome news that MV motorcycles were to be imported into Britain by the newly-created MV Distributors Ltd, headed by Ron Harris, a former Brooklands and Manx Grand Prix road racer, operating from premises in Whetstone, London N.20. The first consignment of machines had already arrived and the MVs were already on display when the ad appeared. Three models were available, all road-going singles, a pushrod 125 and two chain-driven ohc 175s.

With the 250cc and 125cc World Championships under their belt, MV decided to go all out for the prestigious 500cc title. They made sure of this by signing John Surtees, who narrowly missed taking the 350cc title as well. But this was no time to rest on their laurels, as the coming year would show. Meanwhile, MV distributors seized the opportunity to add two more models to the range available in Britain, both 175cc competition models.

In 1957, MV had to fight very hard indeed in a vain attempt to retain any of their World titles. Mondial took the 125cc and 250cc titles, thanks to the efforts of Provini and Sandford, respectively. Moto Guzzi again clung on to the 350cc title, and Gilera just had the edge in the 500cc class. But there was hardly time to do much to stop this onslaught because most of the world's leading manufacturers decided to withdraw from racing before the 1958 season opened. Gilera, Moto Guzzi, Mondial and Norton were amongst the signatories and for the next three years MV went it alone, taking all four World Championship titles. In some respects it was a hollow victory, although much useful information about the frame design, suspension, brakes and riding position was being derived from the racing experience gained. Like his predecessor, the late Les Graham, John Surtees was also a gifted rider and development engineer, who was gradually transforming the fours into machines that were much less difficult to ride. Vic Willoughby, the doyen of all racing riders-cum-journalists could attest to the dubious handling aspects of the fours after he had the opportunity to try a 500 at Monza, after the Italian Grand Prix.

Sadly, the importation of the MV singles had made little or no impact on the British market, with the result that MV Distributors relinquished their franchise during 1959. But MV had not gone for good, as far as this country was concerned. When the factory announced a 150cc scooter, Scooter and Continental Imports of Swedenborg Square, London, E.1., decided to handle it along with the four-strokes.

By 1961, John Surtees had decided to retire from motorcycle

racing so that he could devote more time to his growing interest in racing cars. This left only a young and as yet not too well known Gary Hocking to take his place. A Rhodesian, like Ray Amm, Gary had been runner-up for the 125, 250 and 350cc World titles from virtual obscurity, so he carried a heavy responsibility on his shoulders. Yet he took the 500cc title in 1961 in a devastating manner, winning the German, French, Dutch, Belgian, East German and Swedish Grands Prix. During the course of this he had to meet a very determined challenge from Mike Hailwood, who was riding a very quick Norton! He took the 350cc title too, winning four of the seven qualifying rounds. Strangely enough, the factory lost much prestige during the 1961 season by making what many considered to be a serious blunder. They decided to go through the farce of entering Gary as a private owner, even to the extent of sticking a label marked 'MV Privat' on each side of the fuel tank. It fooled no one, for the works mechanics were always in evidence and easily recognised.

The death of his close friend, Tom Phillis, in the 1962 TT, caused Gary to retire from road racing after his victory in the Senior race. This and a ride in the Junior race had marked his only appearance in the classics that year. It was a double tragedy that soon after his return home, Gary too lost his life, whilst competing in the Natal Grand Prix, having succumbed to the temptation of a seat in a racing car.

Now only Mike Hailwood was available to keep the flag flying, Mike having signed for MV at the end of the 1961 season. With someone like Mike at the helm, it came as no surprise that MV claimed the 500cc World title for 1962 and the three years that were to follow. For good measure, Mike also took the Hour Record at Daytona during 1964, when he recorded 144.82mph on his 500cc four.

On paper at least, 1966 should have been the best season of all, for Giacomo Agostini had joined MV from Morini, to partner Mike in the 1965 title hunt. But this dynamic pairing was not to last. Problems with a new 420cc three-cylinder racer had sidelined Mike on too many occasions. He was lured away by Honda in 1966 and Giacomo had to go it alone using the new three-cylinder 350 and 500 models. The honours were evenly split that year, Mike taking the 350cc title and Giacomo the 500. In 1967 the end result was similar, although MV had the edge on this occasion by taking both the 500cc riders' and manufacturers' titles. But Mike had no chance to level the scores in 1968, as Honda had decided to pull out of racing. In consequence, MV once again found themselves with little or no opposition and took the 500cc and 350cc World Championships for the next five years. This afforded ample opportunity to bring the new 350 and 500cc three-cylinder models to a high standard of reliability and competitiveness. But the writing was on the wall for all to see, Yamaha and Kawasaki having set their sights on the 350 and 500cc titles for the future.

In Britain, MV enthusiasts welcomed the news that MVs were again to be imported, this time by Gus Kuhn Motors Limited, of Stockwell, London, S.W.6. A 600cc four-cylinder, road-going version of the racing fours had been available in Italy since 1965, but a combination of little or no marketing expertise and rather off-putting styling did little to encourage demand from overseas, apart from the high retail price. Some restyling over the two years that followed helped give the machine more appeal, but it was not until the 743cc version became available in 1969 that the export potential began to look promising. Launched initially at the 1971 Milan Show, the 750 Super Sport, as it was then designated, followed and was alleged to have a maximum speed of 160mph and to produce 78bhp. In many respects it more closely resembled its racing counterparts, apart from the use of shaft final drive. It was expected to sell for around the £1600 mark in Britain, a significant increase over the £1000 the earlier 600cc four would have cost when it reached our shores. A four-stroke parallel twin scrambler of 350cc capacity was marketed at the same time, a machine fitted with lighting equipment that would be classified as a 'street scrambler' in the USA. With good ground clearance and an engine/gear unit that formed part of the frame structure, a particularly distinctive feature was the two upswept exhaust pipes and tapering megaphone silencers that ran parallel to each other on the right-hand side. Attractive-looking for that era, it clearly had little chance of competing successfully against the two-stroke-engined machines that were carrying all before them at that time. It was the 750 four that took all the limelight. Yet for all that, the year ended on a sad note, for Count Domenico Agusta, the founder and driving force behind the factory, had died in Milan.

Gus Kuhn Motors continued to import MVs in small numbers until 1974, when they took up the option of becoming the sole UK concessionaires. By this time the 750 Super Sports model had been discontinued and replaced by the restyled 750S model, which soon had an improved design of cylinder head. Now the UK price had risen to £2200, although included with each machine was a kit that permitted the performance to be further uprated, and a race-type fairing. An entirely new 350cc twin was also available, both models being on display for the first time in Britain at the Racing and Sporting Motor Cycle Show held during January that year. In point of fact, purchasers had a choice of two fours, the Sport and the Sport Special. The earlier 750 models were being discounted at something like £400 under list price, to make way for the new designs.

For the 1973 season, Phil Read had joined MV to partner Agostini, the objective being to retain the 350cc and 500cc World Championship titles. It proved to be another outstanding partnership, Agostini taking the 350cc title and Read the 500 at the end of the season. But just as in the case of the earlier dynamic pairing of Hailwood and Agostini, so the new partnership was destined not to last. Before the 1974 season started, Agostini had quit MV to ride for Yamaha, leaving Read to channel all his eforts into retaining the 500 title. This he succeeded in doing, the result being exactly as in the preceding year apart from the fact that Agostini's 350 had 'Yamaha' on the tank. Unbeknown to anyone, this was to be the last world title that MV would take. Yamaha and Suzuki had their sights on the bigger capacity World Championship titles and from now on the Japanese manufacturers would dominate the end of season results, except in the very smallest capacities.

Towards the end of 1975, Gus Kuhm Motors terminated their agreement with the Italian factory as sales of the road-going models had failed to match up to their expectations, even in the case of the 750 fours. Once again, MV had no direct representation in Britain. In Italy, Phil Read had decided to remain with MV, but his efforts to retain the 500 title for a further year were in vain. The factory itself was in anything but good shape, a number of factors having brought about a general decline. Underlying factors were the earlier death of the founder, the instability of the Italian Government and the country's ailing economy, and the company's complete indifference to the impact being made to Japanese motorcycles in overseas markets. Only sponsorship by Elf Petroleum and then by Api had kept the racing going. When matters came to a head it looked at one time as though the factory would cease production completely, but fortunately the situation was retrieved a little when the Italian Government took a controlling interest. As soon as this had been confirmed, an announcement was made to the effect that MVs would continue in production for a minimum of 15 years and that the development of an entirely new flat-four engine was already well under way. It was expected that the prototype would make its debut at the 1977 Milan Show, held during November. Yet even if these measures were to give little more than a stay of execution, the initial message was one of hope at the time when it was most needed.

Encouraged by the news and the emergence of the new 790cc road-going 750S America model, Agusta Concessionaires (GB) Limited took up the MV franchise for Britain, operating initially from premises at Farnham Common, near Slough, in Buckinghamshire. Now only three models were available, the 750S America, an 832cc version known as the 'Boxer' (later changed to 'Monza'), and the 350cc 'Sport Twin'. The America seemed to have a good potential in the USA too, where large capacity machines have always been a traditional requirement. But sadly, the mood of optimism soon changed. The Italian Government had also taken a controlling interest in Ducati, another company with a strong racing background that found itself in difficulties, and it took only another directive to place

Ducati in charge of all future MV motorcycle production. With limited financial resources, all racing had to stop, and this proved to be the *coup de grace* as far as MV was concerned. A combination of very limited production, failure to penetrate overseas markets and an outlook of general complacency all mitigated heavily against the continuation of motorcycle manufacture. MV had now come to the end of the road and would henceforth concentrate all their efforts in the manufacture of helicopters for which they had acquired a sound reputation in the world of aviation.

The legacy MV left behind them was quite remarkable and it will be a long time before any other manufacturer can rival the level of success they attained on the race tracks of the World. In the 25 years from 1952 to 1976, MV Agusta had won 38 individual (riders') World Championships and 37 manufacturers' World Championships. This involved winning 270 World Championship races, some of them for many years in succession. Taking into account other races not of World Championship status, it has been calculated that over 4,000 had been won by MVs during that glorious 25 years period. The individual World Championship listing is as follows:

Year	Capacity class	Rider	Total of Championships (Rider and Manufacturer)
1952	125cc	C. Sandford	2
1953	125cc	C. Sandford	1
1955	125cc	C. Ubbiali	
	250cc	C. Ubbiali	3
1956	125cc	C. Ubbiali	
	250cc	C. Ubbiali	6
	500cc	J. Surtees	
1958	125cc	C. Ubbiali	
	250cc	T. Provini	
	350cc	J. Surtees	8
	500cc	J. Surtees	
1959	125cc	C. Ubbiali	
	250cc	C. Ubbiali	
	350cc	J. Surtees	8
	500cc	J. Surtees	
1960	125cc	C. Ubbiali	
	250cc	C. Ubbiali	
	350cc	J. Surtees	8
	500cc	J. Surtees	
1961	350cc	G. Hocking	
	500cc	G. Hocking	4
1962	500cc	M. Hailwood	2
1963	500cc	M. Hailwood	2
1964	500cc	M. Hailwood	2
1965	500cc	M. Hailwood	2
1966	500cc	G. Agostini	1
1967	500cc	G. Agostini	2
1968	350cc	G. Agostini	
	500cc	G. Agostini	4
1969	350cc	G. Agostini	
	500cc	G. Agostini	4
1970	350cc	G. Agostini	
	500cc	G. Agostini	4
1971	350cc	G. Agostini	
	500cc	G. Agostini	4
1972	350cc	G. Agostini	
	500cc	G. Agostini	4
1973	350cc	G. Agostini	
	500cc	P. Read	3
1974	500cc	P. Read	1
Total		**38**	**75**

With the collapse of MV, Agusta Concessionaires (GB) Limited were forced to close down towards the end of 1978, after unsuccessful negotiations to take over the manufacturing rights and continue manufacture of the road-going models. Others made similar efforts, sadly with no success. Yet even now the spirit of MV lives on. There is talk of a very limited number of 1000cc fours being made in Germany, under the direction and general guidance of Arturo Magni, the former MV Race Team Manager who had served more than 25 years with the factory. Although it is impossible to mention the names of all those closely associated with MV's race track successes, Arturo is the exception. A gifted and highly skilled engineer, he became an integral part of the MV story, ultimately lending his name to a specially tuned 862cc version of the road-going four. When the factory finally shut its doors, Arturo set up his own business close to Milan, specialising in tuning kits for the road models. There could not have been any better endorsement of the quality of these kits.

In Britain, the MV fours live on through the MV Agusta Owners Club, the organisation that acquired all the assets of Agusta Concessionaires (GB) Limited when the latter closed down. Their display is a certain crowd puller at the classic bike shows and exhibitions, as is the appearance of any of the 'works' four-cylinder racers at a race track or special parade. In these days of the screaming two-stroke, the roar of an MV four in full song has a fatal attraction for old and young alike. The old magic is still there ....

EVOLUTION

When the first of the road-going four-cylinder MVs appeared during 1965, it could have been expected to create quite an impact on the motorcycling world. Right from the early pioneer days, a four-cylinder motorcycle has always had a strange attraction, even if it proved expensive compared with its contemporaries and was beyond the means of the average rider. One of the first was the Binks in-line four, made in Nottingham soon after the turn of the century. Other designs followed, such as the FN, Pierce Arrow, Henderson, Indian Ace and the Ariel Square Four. With one or two exceptions, most bore no particular allegiance to racing models, mainly because multi-cylinder racers were quite uncommon outside the USA. So the MV broke new ground in this respect, by representing an attempt to make an over-the-counter version of the Grand Prix racers for the man in the street — at a price.

Somehow the opportunity was missed, for instead of appearing in the brilliant fire engine red that was so characteristic of the racing MVs, the newcomer made its debut in sombre black. It looked ungainly in several respects, the somewhat gross-looking fuel tank having the appearance of the early Japanese 'back to front' designs. With chrome-plated sides and a

black centre strip, it was relieved only by the MV motif and a pair of stick-on knee grips. The tank also seemed to tower above the two-level dualseat, which possessed no hump at the rear.

Of conventional design, the telescopic front forks carried a large, ugly, rectangular headlamp, which projected well forward and had the instruments recessed into the top. High rise handlebars were fitted. The front brake was of the twin disc type, operated by cable. The frame was of the duplex tube type, the rear end having a swinging arm of conventional type, controlled by two hydraulic suspension units. A crash bar protected the engine unit at the front. Only the engine/gear unit could be closely identified with the racing engine, although even this illusion was spoilt by the use of only two carburetters and by having the two exhaust pipes on each side terminate in a single cylindrical silencer. The mudguards were painted black, the front one being edged with a chromium-plated strip along the leading edge. The rear mudguard carried two rectangular toolboxes, one mounted on each side. The rear brake was of the drum type, final drive being by shaft and bevel pinions.

Like the racing engine, the engine unit of the road-going model was inclined forward in the frame at an angle of 20° and was of the dohc type, using a gear pinion drive between the middle cylinders. To arrive at a capacity of 592cc, the bore and stroke dimensions had been increased to 58 x 56mm. Having two 24mm Dell'Orto carburetters and a compression ratio of 9.3:1, 50bhp was available at 8200rpm. A starter of the dynamotor type was used in lieu of a kickstarter.

The gearbox was of the five-speed type, the unit-construction primary drive being via a multiplate clutch. Both wheels were of 18 inch diameter, the front wheel having a tyre of 3.50 inch section and the rear wheel one of 4 inch.

The front brake discs were of 216mm diameter, and the rear drum brake of 200mm.

Dimension-wise, the machine had a wheelbase of 139cm, a length of 221cm and a width of 81cm. It weighed 221kg. Maximum speed was 177kph (110mph).

Very few of these machines found their way into Britain, although one was featured as a prize in a competition run by *Motor Cycle News*. Much to the disgust of those who hoped they had completed the successful entry, the winner proved to be a sidecar enthusiast, who promptly attached a third wheel. This, it seemed, was the ultimate degradation!

It took some time for the factory to realise that there would be a much better spin-off from the racing models if their road-going counterparts were restyled to look more like them. The main purchaser was, after all, one who had a decidedly sporting instinct and who would most probably have been influenced by MV's racing successes. It was not until late 1969 that the completely restyled version appeared, by which time the capacity had been raised to 743cc by increasing the bore size to 65mm. This, and the use of four 24mm carburetters increased the power output to 69bhp at 8900rpm. More noticeable changes in specifications included a more shapely fuel tank with blue sidepanels and a white flash, a red enamelled frame and a dualseat covered in red material, with a hump at the end, much sleeker-looking Ceriani telescopic front forks with a separate chrome-plated headlamp mounted on projecting lugs, and exhaust pipes that terminated in long, tapering, megaphone-type silencers, two on each side of the machine. In addition, the two mechanically-operated front disc brakes had been replaced by massive twin drum brakes, whilst the handlebars were now of the clip-on racing type, with closed ends that projected beyond the grips. The effect was both instant and dramatic – one wondered why it had taken MV almost five years to capitalise on their racing successes by doing what seemed so obvious!

The first of the 743cc models was imported into Britain during October 1972, at the time when Gus Kuhn Motors had started to take an interest in the fours. The basic model was designated the 750GT, there being the option of a somewhat similar model, but with sports styling, the 750S. Imports of the 750GT model continued until November 1973, by which time only the 750S model was available. Just over a year later, in January 1974, the 750S had the benefit of an improved cylinder head, commencing with engine number 2140418. Imports of the 750S model finally ceased during September 1975, by which time an improved 790cc four was in production.

The 790cc model continued the '750S' designation but with the addition of the name 'America', which reflects the country in which it was expected to have particularly good sales. But with a six thousand dollar price tag, it represented a very expensive acquisition, and with only 200 expected to be shipped from Italy each year, the prospect of good sales never materialised. Essential differences between the America and its predecessors were the restyled fuel tank, now finished in red and relieved only by a broad silver band on each side, immediately below the MV decal. The lines of the tank were accentuated by side panels, which masked the space between the carburetter intakes and the top of the rear suspension units, the top of the panels blending in with the base of the black-coloured dualseat. The megaphone-shaped silencers, two on each side, were now shorter and had reverse cone ends, so that they more closely resembled their racing counterparts. The effect was enhanced by a matt black crackle

finish. A useful feature was an adjustable end to the dualseat, so that it could be adapted for either solo or pillion use. The headlamp was also finished in a matt black and the tachometer and speedometer had shallower holders, with the same black crackle finish.

The increase in engine capacity had been achieved by a further increase in bore size, this time by 2mm to give bore and stroke measurements of 67 x 56mm. With a compression ratio of 9.5:1, the power output was raised to 86bhp at 8500rpm, with maximum torque at 7500rpm. This permitted a maximum speed in the region of 220kph (137mph), the dry weight of the machine being 253kg (562lb). Two versions were available, the '750S America' being supplied with steel wheel rims and a 10 inch diameter rear drum brake. The alternative '750S America DX' model was supplied with alloy wheel rims and had a rear disc brake. Both models had twin front disc brakes and continued in production until February 1979.

A larger capacity version of the America models, but built to the same basic specification, became available in Britain during July 1977. This model had an engine capacity of 832cc, brought about by increasing the bore size by a further two millimetres. For reasons unknown, this was designated the 'Boxer' model, an unfortunate choice of name because it implied the engine was of the flat-four type (with which the factory was experimenting) which most certainly was not the case. This name persisted until February 1978, when it was replaced by the much more suitable choice of 'Monza'. Ferrari had objected as they had prior right to the name 'Boxer' for one of their cars. There was no alternative to the alloy wheel rims with which the machine was supplied, or the rear disc brake. Separate choke controls were, however, used in conjunction with the carburetters. Like the Americas,

the Monza ceased production during February 1979.

Even the Monza was not the largest capacity road-going four to become available from the factory. For the owner who required the ultimate in performance, an 862cc version became available during April 1978, known as the 'Monza Arturo Magni'. It differed from the standard Monza model by having 30mm carburetters, a further increase in bore size to 70mm, and an all-black exhaust of the traditional four pipe layout. What was referred to as a 'competition rev counter' replaced the type of tachometer that had been supplied as a standard fitment in the past. It goes without saying that the Monza Arturo Magni had a specially-tuned engine: this aspect of the machine having been supervised by the great man himself. This model, too, came to an end when production of motorcycles finally drew to a close in February 1979. It seems particularly fitting that one of the last MV models made should pay tribute to the name of the man who gave MVs so many of their racing successes.

The final fling occurred during late 1978 when the largest of all the road-going fours made the headlines. This was the 955cc 'Ago', named after Giacomo Agostini and based on the 1978 'Corona' model he had ridden in the over 750cc class at Imola. With the bore size already stretched to 70mm, the stroke was increased to 62mm to give the necessary increase in cubic capacity. Running at a 10:1 compression ratio, and with 30mm Dell'Orto carburetters fitted with accelerator pumps, the Ago produced 99bhp at 10,200rpm. Similar in most respects to the other road-going fours, the Ago had one or two interesting features, not all of which were evident. Whilst the left-hand frame downtube and under-section could be detached to make removal and re-installation of the engine unit easier to accomplish, it was not so evident that the inside of the crankcase castings had been painted with a filler paint to stop oil sweat as a result of porosity. Furthermore, to increase rigidity of the frame, the upper tubes that joined the steering head assembly had been sleeved. For all this, the new model was claimed to be lighter in weight than its predecessors and to have a lower centre of gravity than the standard America. But sadly, comparatively few of these models were made before the factory closed its doors for good as far as the manufacture of motorcycles was concerned. The MV four, in its many guises, had finally reached the end of the line.

As may be expected, MV fours have acquired a collectors' value and good examples are quite difficult to obtain. The MV Agusta Owners Club has a total of 91 fours on record as being owned in Britain, although it is believed there may be as many as 150 since some owners are not members of the club, or perhaps even aware of its existence.

SPECIFICATION

790cc 750S America model

For supplementary information on other models see 'Evolution' section.

Engine

Four cylinder in-line mounted transversely across the frame. Cast iron cylinder liners in aluminium alloy barrels with aluminium alloy cylinder head. DOHC valve gear driven by gear pinions between middle cylinders. Primary drive by helical gears to gearbox built in-unit with engine.

Capacity: 789.7cc.
Compression ratio 9.5:1.
Bore and stroke: 67x56mm.
Power output: 75bhp at 8500rpm.
Maximum torque: 6.62kgm at 7500rpm.

Gearbox

Built in-unit with engine. Drive by helical gears. Final drive by Carden shaft to the rear wheel. 5-speed positive stop with foot-operated gear change. Ratios: 1st 11.84:1, 2nd 8.4:1, 3rd 6.36:1, 4th 5.52:1 and 5th 4.97:1.

Clutch

Multiple plate type.

Lubrication

Force feed by gear-type oil pump. System protected by mesh filter and changeable filter element. Oil contained in crankcase compartment (6.6 pints).

Exhaust system

Four separate exhaust pipes and four tapered megaphone-type straight through silencers. Two on each side of machine.

Carburetters

Four Dell'Orto type VHB 26.

Ignition system

Coil and single contact breaker, using Bosch Type JF4 distributor. Champion N-3 sparking plugs.

Frame

Duplex tube cradle type with swinging arm controlled by adjustable hydraulic suspension units.

Forks

Ceriani telescopic forks with hydraulic damping.

Wheels

Alloy rims with laced-up hubs. Both rims 18 inch diameter.

Brakes

Twin Scarab or Brembo discs at front, hydraulically-operated. Rear, 10 inch diameter drum brake centrally disposed in wheel.

Tyres

Front: 3.50 x 18 inch, with ribbed tread pattern. Rear: 4.00 x 18 inch with racing style block tread. Metzeler manufacture.

Electrical system

12 volt. Electric engine starter of the dynamotor type. Stoplamp switch fitted to front and rear brakes. Battery 12 volt, 32 amp hour. Generator 12 volt with 135 watt maximum output.

Dimensions and weight

Dry weight: 253kg (562lb).
Length: 211cm (83.0in).
Wheelbase: 139cm (54.7in).

ROAD TESTS

MV AGUSTA SPORT AMERICA
Getting the adrenalin flowing

OVERWORKED and somehow inadequate words like Character and Presence and Charisma tend to recur in conversations during chance meetings of enthusiasts on the road when the focus of discussion is an MV Agusta 750 Sport America. It gets the adrenalin flowing even when hunched in silent majesty on the stand and it is interesting to see the effect it has on people who would not normally give a motorcycle a second glance. City gents in bowlers cross over — nonchalantly, that is, for it would never do to appear impatient to examine such an obviously rorty device and care must be taken to preserve a civilized image. Then, if the rider is near and looks as if he might be a reasonable sort, one or two polite observations may be in order, like, "A fine looking machine you have there." While a bolder spirit anxious to demonstrate that, dash it all, he does know something about it, may venture, "Raced, weren't they, years ago?" or perhaps — "Surely that fellow Surtees did well on them — yes, knew I was right!" Approve of what it does and what it represents or not, an MV is difficult to ignore and that applied with particular force to the machine borrowed for test. It was loud.

This Four, the personal bike of Italian specialist dealer Mike Ward of Nottingham, is to the same general specification as the last of the line available up to 12 months ago save for the incorporation of optional components which convert a standard model to Monza state of tune. It looks a battle-scarred veteran for a machine with just a few thousand miles behind it but that is perhaps not surprising in view of its history. It had a hard life before Ward got it.

MV Concessionaires of Slough had apparently used it for Press demonstrations/road tests and it bears many signs of rough treatment for engine inspection plugs have chisel marks, chipped paint at the front of the tank indicates that it has been carelessly removed at some time, large alloy nuts on the forks are scored and lower engine covers grazed. Ward believes it was dropped before he got it.

He noticed it looking forlorn and covered in dust in a corner behind the concessionaire's premises about a year ago when rumours that the Italians were halting motorcycle production were hardening into fact. Ward, realizing that he had to act quickly if he wanted a Four of his own before supplies dried up, put in a bid and got it without much trouble as by then nobody at Slough seemed very bothered what happened to it and shortly afterwards speculation was confirmed: MVs were indeed retrenching to concentrate on helicopters and other work. There would be no more motor bikes.

Despite its chequered past, the MV remains a scintillating performer. The magnificent engine is vibrationless, the gearbox among the best, transmission hard to fault and the disc front brakes are awesomely powerful. The engine makes all the right noises, music to an enthusiast's ear. These days it takes something special to get me out of bed at six in the morning. The MV did. On test it covered 1,035 miles in four days. It was hard to keep off it. It was a privilege to be allowed to ride it far and fast without restraint and I made the most of my time with it and thoroughly enjoyed the experience.

The 750 Sport America, which bears a striking resemblance to the 500 cc racing fours of the early 1950s, was offered in various forms in the five or six years it was available in Britain. Early 750 Fours had classic, timeless lines with rounded tanks, a dumpy racing-type single-seat and matching "toolboxes," which doubled as battery covers. Subsequent re-styling altered tank shape and introduced louvred side panels which, taking the place of "toolboxes" hid the battery. In all essentials, the specification of engine, gearbox and transmission was the same for all models, though overbored cylinders, alternative camshafts and carburettors and different wheels and brakes were obtainable for later machines.

There is some uncertainty about the antecedents of the frame, a duplex downtube cradle type with distinctive humped top tube to permit engine removal, but it is generally

MEN OF EXPERIENCE

I MUST record my thanks to three other MV owners, all men with considerable experience of motorcycles, for help and advice when this MV report was being prepared.

Not entirely happy with the roadholding of Mike Ward's MV, I asked former world champion roadracer Bill Lomas, now a dealer with shops at Milford and Clay Cross in Derbyshire, what he thought of the roadholding of his personal machine, an 832 cc Arturo Magni version. His bike, which had then done less than a third of the recommended running-in mileage of 1,800, has Metzlers, a dolphin fairing, chamois-finished single seat and Koni shock absorbers but is in most other respects similar to the test machine.

Lomas, who is still, 20 or so years on from his racing days no slow-coach whatever he rides, described his bike's grip on dry roads as "all right". Pressed, he said that it does "wobble a bit" and thinks the handbook recommendations on tyre pressures . . . suggested minimum settings are 28 lpsi front, 34 rear . . . too high and prefers 24/28.

Son Mike, who tries to keep his Yamaha RD400 close behind the MV on a run, said he has noticed that in bends the MV "snakes a bit." Bill Lomas favours Dunlop TT100s, which have apparently improved the stability of various sports machines used on ordinary

roads, though to date he has found neither opportunity nor real reason to change from Metzlers.

Estate agent Richard Marchant of Holcot, Northants, another MV Four owner, rode the test machine from Oakham to Melton Mowbray on dry roads while I followed on his 900 Super Sport Desmo Ducati. There was no hanging about and afterwards Marchant said he had found the MV's roadholding "acceptable" and no different from his own bike's. He also thought Ward's bike had more torque and said it seemed quicker. Moving straight from the MV, I thought the big Ducati's roadholding was much better; it stayed put in the most convincing manner and could be placed exactly were desired in the certain knowledge that it would hold course no matter what. It was inspiring. There was plenty of mechanical clatter below 60 mph but above that speed the din was carried away on the wind. A very impressive machine, with good brakes and gearbox.

Another educational interlude occurred when Nottinghamshire building contractor Bill Moore allowed me a spin on his immaculate, and standard, 750 Sport America, which had then clocked up precisely 800 miles. This bike, tried over winding back roads, was definitely more stable over bumps; the steering had a tauter feel than the test bike's and on

indifferently-surfaced roads wobbling at speed was milder. I found it the preferable bike of the two.

Moore echoed my findings after trying the test machine and remarked on its low-speed "wander" and weaving when going fast; I gather its behaviour never alarmed him but he concluded that it could be improved. His MV has Metzlers and the standard Sebac rear units and he commented: "You must go purposefully into a bend, not on a neutral throttle, with the MV; I think its cornering ability is then very good at medium speed. My bike feels more secure than the test machine and I shouldn't be surprised to learn Ward's bike has been down the road. . . ."

Ward's workshop mechanic Trevor Milner, who has ridden many of the large-capacity machines now available, believes that high engine mass, inevitable with the transverse-four layout, is responsible for causing speed wobble and has found that a Laverda Triple is also susceptible. In his experience, big twins like the Guzzi Le Mans and Ducati vees do not wobble. Milner commented: "With the MV 750 you must go hard into bends. Don't be half-hearted. Keep the power on and it feels very good. Being gentle with the twistgrip starts it wobbling. I have found that all the transverse fours I have tried will roll from side to side in certain conditions and I put the effect down to high and wide engines."

believed to be the same as that made for the 600 cc Tourer of the mid-1960s. An all-black Tourer, a model very rare in this country, was seen in the Isle of Man during TT week some years ago. Reports suggest it was a dilettante's plaything and an expensive disappointment.

The 750 Sport America, compared with other high-performance bikes of similar capacity, still looks dear on paper now (this report was compiled in September 1979) but the engine shows evidence of much costly refinement and selective assembly, which help to explain the

price. With crankcase and transmission covers off and innards exposed, the engine is seen to be a work of art typical of Italian engineering craftsmanship at its finest. Though other manufacturers of large-capacity Fours follow accepted practice in running valves direct in

MV 850 as produced in 1977 and advertised by the English concessionaires as "The world's fastest-ever production motorcycle". On the open road, it was said (by the concessionaries' PR people), to shrug off even the most persistent of the so-called superbikes with gears to spare. The price was given as £3,973, going up to "well over £4,000" when fitted with the optional fairing

It has been estimated that only 50 Fours were sold here

Another variation: the 750 GT roadster as sold by Gus Kuhn of South London

cylinder heads, MVs specified separate, cast-iron, detachable troughs to carry guides and valves. Should gearbox or transmission give trouble, they can be dismantled in situ, leaving the engine undisturbed. Experienced British consultant engineers who examined the MV's specification called it poetry in metal, applauded the Gallarate designers and asked how on earth the factory expected to make a profit from what was, in Japanese terms, a very small number of machines. It has been estimated that only 50 Fours were sold here.

Similarities with the early racing MV Fours, which were based on a Gilera design, are immediately obvious in the 750 Sport America: gear-driven twin overhead camshafts, helical gear primary drive, aluminium-alloy cylinder barrels and heads inclined forward 20 degrees, apparently identical engine/gearbox castings, a massive and generously finned sump and ignition distributor angled backwards between the inner carburettors.

With detachable side panels in place to cover the gap between carburettor trumpets and mudguard, the MV presents a profile of frame packed with power, and flowing lines and graceful exhaust pipes bewitch the eye. Viewed head on, the MV resembles a charging bull and bristles with menace. Creating an impression of terrific speed even at rest, it remains unequalled for sporting good looks.

In 750 Sport America form, the aircooled transverse four-cylinder four-stroke has bore and stroke dimensions of 67 mm × 56 mm, 9.5:1 compression ratio, cast-iron liners shrunk into the barrels and a one-piece cylinder head with V-mounted valves operated by caps and plungers.

MV Agusta claimed a maximum power output of 75 bhp at 8,500 rpm, achieved with valve timing as follows: intake opens 48 degrees before top dead centre, closes 68 degrees after bottom dead centre; exhaust opens 70 degrees before top dead centre, closes 36 degrees after top dead centre. Valve clearances, with a cold engine, are the same for intake and exhaust — 12 thou. Maximum torque is said to be 47.9 ft-lb (6.62 kgm) at 7,500 rpm. There was some doubt about the cubic capacity of the test machine but

it was thought to be slightly bigger than the original 743 cc Four.

A built-up crankshaft comprising five pieces has six main bearings, four roller-type and two ball races. A pinion between numbers one and two cranks on the nearside drives a primary transmission gear and another, smaller pinion between the middle cylinders drives the camshaft gear train which runs in a removable tunnel, a gear-type oil pump provides pressure lubrication for the inner four crankshaft bearings, the others being splash-lubricated from the sump.

Oil is drawn into the pump through a mesh filter at the bottom of the sump and passes through a second filter, with replaceable cartridge, in the distribution line. This has a by-pass valve which operates if the filter becomes clogged; it then closes off the filter section and passes oil straight into the

---

ASIDES . . .

MV information sheets, urging careful running-in, advised that during its first 600 miles a 750 Four should not be taken above the following speeds in the gears: first, 32 mph (5,000), second, 45 mph (5,000), third, 64 mph (5,500), fourth, 76 mph (5,700), top, 90 mph (6,000). Between 600 and 1,800 miles recommended maxima were: first, 38 mph (6,000), second, 53 mph (6,000), third, 70 mph (6,000), fourth, 90 mph (6,500), top, 106 mph (7,000).

With a fully run-in engine, the makers said a 750 Four was mechanically safe to 9,000 rpm in all gears and quoted speeds as follows: first, 57 mph; second, 80 mph; third, 105 mph; fourth, 125 mph; top, 135 mph; the rev-counter being redlined between 9,500 and 11,000.

The final retail price list, issued by MV Concessionaires at Slough on 15 April, 1978, was as follows: Monza 861 cc Arturo Magni Special with wire wheels £4,498, with mag. wheels £4,927.99. Monza 832 cc with wire wheels £3,457, with mags. £3,887. 750 Sport America (789 cc engine) with wire wheels £3,187, with mags £3,617. The last batch manufactured all had disc front brakes, the double-sided twin-leading-shoe braked wheel having been discontinued two or three years earlier.

An admitted weak point on all the Fours was the clutch, surprisingly small for the

power it had to transmit. It was strongly rumoured that the clutch was being improved when factory executives decided to halt motorcycle production. It is possible to convert any of the roadgoing Fours to chain drive.

A conversion kit, extremely expensive, comprised front and rear sprockets, different engine/gearbox covers, alternative swinging-arm and wheel, and of course a chain. It is alleged the cost was close on £1,000. A very rapid MV so converted has appeared in long-distance races on the Continent recently.

Many extras were available at one time or another; the most popular was a beautifully-tailored and very slim dolphin fairing. Three stages of tune were also offered to owners of standard 750 Fours. It is estimated that an MV fitted with every possible extra would have cost approximately £7,000 ex-works.

To assist with maintenance, a second main stand was available; it enabled both wheels to be raised clear of the ground. A comprehensive Official Workshop Manual (retail price, £25.00) and a separate Official Spares List, both produced to the same high standard, both in English, were also available.

How many of the Fours sold here were bought by private owners? Bill Lomas thinks very few. Most, he believes, passed into

trade hands. Although I should emphasise that Lomas did not suggest this, there were, it appears, always doubts about the long-term prospects of a good spares supply. This factor may well have influenced private individuals, not in a position to pull strings if things got tough, to settle for more popular machines. Hence the comparatively small number of MVs sold in Britain.

And now an appeal. As regular readers may have guessed, *Motorcycle Sport* is not run by folk with money to burn. Therefore the kind of ultra-sophisticated analytical apparatus much favoured by free-spending American journals is beyond reach; in any case, I am not at all sure it is really necessary.

One facility, however, is: a suitable venue where a machine's *true* top speed may be determined. If one or two other points of interest, such as braking distance from 30 mph and 60 mph and acceleration from rest can be recorded at the same time, so much the better. Please don't suggest the MIRA ground at Lindley in the Midlands; that is already rather too well patronized and journalists thrive on "exclusives".

I am keenly aware that this report shows a dearth of hard facts: here, dear reader, is your chance to help *Motorcycle Sport's* contributors to put more meat into their critiques in future. No heavy fees, of course, but doubtless a jar or two would be in order. Offers, then, to the usual address . . .

distribution line. Force-fed oil lubricates gudgeon pins, needle bearings at the small ends, pistons and barrels. It then passes to the cylinder head where it is delivered via holes to the camshafts and by ducts to the cams. Oil drains back to the sump and crankshaft motion splash-lubricates gearbox shafts, needle bearings, bushes and pinions. An eight-plate clutch runs in oil mist.

Like a Ferrari or Maserati, the MV burns some oil in the interests of mechanical longevity and on the first start of the day it was noticeable that the test bike, chokes on, smoked. Provided that engine oil filters are cleaned and/or replaced as necessary and the engine oil (six and a half pints) is changed every 3,600 miles as recommended, an MV Four should do a considerable mileage before it requires overhaul.

A separate, secondary gearbox, in tandem with the five-speed box, transmits power through a totally-enclosed shaft running in oil to bevel gears in the rear hub; the shaft housing doubles as the other arm of the pivoted fork, which is controlled by five position Sebac hydraulically-damped spring units with hand adjusters to alter the spring rate. Overall gearbox ratios are 11.84:1, 8.40:1, 6.36:1, 5.52:1 and 4.97:1. The swinging-arm pivots on roller bearings.

Four Dell'Orto VHB DD or VHB DS 26 mm carburettors, with choke linkage operated by a lever on the left, draw air through a filter element on a standard 750 Sport America, but the test bike had 27 mm carburettors with individual choke controls and air intake horns in place of the airbox as fitted to the Arturo Magni overbored engine, and a cylinder head reworked to Monza specification. A belt-driven 12V 135W Bosch Dynastarter, Bosch JF4 type distributor and battery and coil ignition supply sparks to the two-valve heads, and no kickstarter is fitted. Total ignition advance is 46 to 50 degrees, firing order 1-3-4-2 and recommended spark plugs are Champion N3 or equivalent.

Night-riding illumination comes from a 7in Aprilia headlamp with 12V 45/40 main bulb, and a biggish 6 × 5in Aprilia red light makes the rear prominent to following traffic. The ignition key works a switch mounted below the tank and there are three positions: On (when the lights may be used), Off and Park, when a 2.5w bulb in the headlamp shell and one rear lamp come on. Four 8-amp fuses protect the different circuits.

Because the 4¼-gallon steel tank has a broad base, the ignition switch is out of sight and awkward to reach from the seat. Handlebar switches by Aprilia had a cheap and tacky feel but worked well, with a logical operating sequence and gave no trouble during the test. Tommaselli dropped bars had black blanking plugs, a neat touch. There was no mirror and Mike Ward had removed the direction indicators and the standard MV single seat; instead the test bike had a good Ducati dualseat which he had modified to suit the MV mountings and everyone who saw the machine agreed that the seat blended well with the bike's lines. Ceriani forks with exposed stanchions, Metzler 350 × 18in front and Avon Roadrunner 4.25 × 18in rear tyres, two 11in cast-iron discs with Scarab calipers behind the fork legs, an 8½in drum cable-operated rear brake and heavy duty Borrani alloy rims complete an impressive specification. Dimensions of Ward's bike, common to all versions, are: wheelbase 55in, seat height 30½in, width 28in, length 79in, overall height 38 in, ground clearance 6in. With

a full petrol tank but no toolkit, which is normally carried in a lockable box faired into the single seat, the MV weighed 539lb.

Before the test began in earnest (when the bike, according to the odometer, had done just 4,433 miles) Mike Ward explained that he had spent a long time checking everything as he was keen to get the best from it. He had stripped the front forks and adjusted the head bearings to a nicety, balanced the carburettors and tuned the ignition as a worn fibre heel on the contact-breaker had upset the timing. Although there were still several jobs he wanted to do, at that point he found performance more than satisfactory and noted that in 500 miles during Manx Grand Prix week the MV averaged 44 mpg and used just under half a pint of SAE40 engine oil.

Starting was invariably a first-time affair. The drill was: flick on outer cold-start levers . . . the inner pair being hard to get at . . . turn on both petrol taps and, given a fraction of throttle, the engine was usually firing on the first touch of the button; only after passing through a ford was the MV slow to respond, water having got onto the driving belt of the starter motor. It was advisable to spend a minute or two warming it up at a steady 2,000 rpm on mornings when air temperature was below 60 deg. F, and indeed the owner's manual warns against riding off straight away as combustion heat spreads slowly through the large alloy engine. As the chill disappeared, the "choke" levers could be turned off but it was as well to go steadily for the first few miles after an overnight stop until the power unit was thoroughly warm.

The MV broadcast its presence. At tickover speeds, which varied for no obvious reason between about 900 revs and 1,600, it growled and chugged like a tractor and in built-up aeas its bellow was embarrassing. Pronounced whirring and clicking sounds were amplified by the deep tank and in traffic this high-stepping thoroughbred chafed impatiently at the bit, eager to be turned loose. When the MV was cramped among slow-moving vehicles, the penetrating exhaust note drew stern looks from constables, and elderly citizens in particular scowled and turned away and there were times when the MV seemed about to become a target for rotten eggs.

There was a different response from the law when the MV passed through a Leicestershire village. Edging forward in a traffic jam, the bike stopped behind a patrol car. The windows were down and two pairs of beady eyes looked for the source of the din. Things looked black when a brawny arm beckoned the MV, which sounded louder than ever, to draw alongside; then a voice commanded, "Keep blipping it . . . we have never seen one before," and it turned out that both crewmen were motorcyclists (Norton 650SS and 150 cc MZ).

Away from suburban speed limits, the MV came into its own. Taken up to 5,000 rpm in the gears as roads cleared, the engine roared with life and felt unburstable and response to the throttle was immediate, strong, smooth. When a motorist misjudged the MV's speed of approach and turned across its path, only the bike's sure and powerful brakes denied the ambulance-men . . .

Banked well over for tight bends, the MV was stable, sure-footed, vicefree but it was plainly less confident on long uneven curves which made it wriggle and it objected strongly to cross-hatchings at junctions and to all other painted surfaces, and cat's-eyes tossed it about; but in slow corners it exhibited no trace of the unnerving top-heaviness experienced on a similar machine tried two years ago.

Chaised metal footrests provided eloquent proof that this classic engine design had been made as smooth as possible without recourse to rubberized mounts, balance shafts, etc, for whatever the MV's speed there was never the slightest sign of vibration through them. In cities only the lower three gears were needed and in hilly Lincoln just the first two. At times the clutch took up the drive in two distinct stages, although the hand lever had been fully released.

Initially I thought the riding position afforded by the drooping bars and footrests a couple of inches behind the seat nose very good but there was a price to pay and two days after collecting the MV and putting 450 miles on it I contracted "MV back" — a malady, little known to medical science, which caused aches and twinges of the lower spine, but happily the trouble cleared up before the test ended.

The headlamp was unexpectedly effective once the shell had been thumped (no tools supplied) to a lower setting and main beam brought down to earth. It threw a brilliant light far enough ahead to warn of potential danger and tricky turns and the pattern was admirable. On a run from Stockport to Buxton one moonless night, the headlamp produced its own genie. A beam intensifier, a bowl-shaped piece of metal, broke free and rolled against the glass, interfering with the shaft of light and blinding oncoming drivers.

Occasionally the engine spat back and banged once or twice when throttled down below 3,000 rpm and it was not really happy in top at about 30 mph when the rev-counter showed 2,500 rpm (the handbook advises against holding it at 2,200 rpm under load).

Twice the sole reason for turning back was the need to reload with fivers. The MV got through a lot of petrol but it was not unbearably thirsty, it seemed, during medium-speed tours of the Lake District, the fen country and The

In concrete canyons the MV was deafening and clearly upset non-believers

Potteries, though some fuel was lost from the Monza-type snapshut filler cap when the level was high; and the twin taps ought to be marked Off-On-Res, made bigger and re-positioned because at full throttle the carburettor linkage brushed them. A rattling noise at the front proved to be nothing serious: just the disc pads chattering in their cups.

Towards the end of the test the clutch slipped, facia warning lights were no bigger than pin heads, Neutral and Generator bulbs flickered weakly and off and on of their own accord, and it was hard to tell when the rear brake was working (it had a long, long cable). The horn was passable.

Wherever the MV was ridden . . . between winding stone walls in the Yorkshire Dales, out over the wide plains along the east coast, high into the Pennines . . . it was hard not to dwell on its racing ancestry. It was, perhaps, an excusable fantasy of a no-hoper that on it he could show the real TT riders a thing or two, for throughout the test echoes of 37 world championships repeatedly intruded on a cool objective appraisal; and there speaks a failed racer. The noise had a lot to do with it. In concrete canyons, it was deafening and clearly upset non-believers and fuelled the arguments of people who equate all motorcycles with unnecessary din and would like to see them banned; these days riders to whom bikes are meat and drink need all the friends they can get. The MV was, more often than not, offensively loud, I regret to say.

It inspired a neat riding style. There was a solid, beefy feel about it and when the leading tyre punched into a crater, nothing protested except me. Only one thing necessary to

Similarities with the early racing MV fours are immediately apparent. No other transverse four has quite the class . . . .

complete the illusion that the MV was screaming round the Island, instead of dawdling in English country lanes, was missing — the smell of "R".

There were no complaints about the choice of ratios. The gearbox change action . . . taken through a rearset linkage on the left . . . was also excellent: short, positive, quick . . . and I could find no fault with the rest of the transmission. The rear wheel bevel box used no oil and none leaked from the shaft drive casing.

It seemed that this was to be another "dry" test in a perplexing summer but the heavens opened and deluged the Midlands a few hours before the MV was due to go back to Ward's Garage (Daybrook) as the bike sped down the M69 near Hinckley. A stiff side wind, very unpredictable, was strong enough to flex panels on tall lorries and gave the MV a hard time as the torrent filled gutters and flooded approach roads but the bike ploughed on at 65-70 mph without too much fuss, though it swayed a fair bit. The MV gave a nicely-cushioned ride which when a passenger was carried became luxurious, and there were no complaints about the accommodation nor the level of comfort from the back seat; the Cerianis looked immensely strong and well up to the job and were correctly sprung for the weight of the machine. Firm when the bike was used one-up, they complemented the action of the rear struts perfectly when the load was increased.

It may have been an aural illusion but I'd swear the right-hand silencers made most noise and at 40 mph in top on a light throttle they made the MV sound like a Mark VIII Velo. When it was travelling faster and had to be shut off while slower traffic got out of the way, the MV produced a thunderous hum.

When Reserve was required, it paid to go 15 or 20 miles before stopping to refill for only then **would the tank accept three gallons. The**

standby supply, incidentally, was good for about 60 miles; much more and one risked a long push to the pumps.

After three or four miles of very slow progress across Birmingham, the bike became temperamental as the tickover fluctuated wildly between 1,000 and 2,000 and one plug played up. Soot coated the silencer outlets but the plugs stayed free of lampblack.

During the test the big Varta battery below the seat became covered in an oily mist of carburettor blow-back but did not require topping up; parking lights were adequate and nothing — apart from the headlamp metal cup — broke or fell off. Although there was no place for tools, Mike Ward had coiled a new clutch cable under the seat. It was not required.

Attempts to see what it would do "on the clock" (see panel) were inconclusive for on reaching 110 mph the speedometer needle refused to go further, though the bike was still accelerating, and the rev-counter needle also seemed reluctant and stuck at 7,900-8,000 rpm . . . some doubt here as both needles were nervous and road shocks also made them twitch. Both "clocks" were Smiths. It was while I was trying for maximum speed that a goggle strap broke, which will mean little to the reader until I add that top-quality elastics have never before failed at speeds up to 130 mph. I tried again with a new strap and that also broke.

Fuel consumption varied between 57 mpg and 31 mpg. A diverting Sunday afternoon was spent making careful checks. The tank was drained and a measured gallon of four-star put in, an emergency half-gallon being carried in a haversack. The MV was kept below 70 mph at all times and taken up the Great North Road. Before gasping to a stop it covered 51.6 miles. It had been cruised at 50-50 mph. When the tiger in the engine was chained up even more securely and speed kept down to 40-50 mph, a similar test produced 56.7 mpg . . . call it 57 because a drop or two was spilled when another measured gallon went in. Unleashed and showing its claws, the MV managed just over 30 mpg and required a pint of engine oil after 550 high-speed miles to bring the level back up to the max. mark on the dipstick.

A few smears of oil stained the engine covers, most notably along a joint below nos. 3 and 4 cylinder barrels and some seeped from a plug on top of the camshaft drive housing. Coming to the bike after it had stood overnight, I noticed one or two drops of oil from an outlet in the nearside lower frame rail (the engine breather vents into the steering head) but there was nothing here to cause real concern.

As the test ended, the MV felt and sounded as crisp and willing as it had at the start and gave the impression that it would continue to deliver the same intoxicating performance for many more thousands of miles while needing little attention beyond periodic topping-up with fuel and oil; although it must be said that a question mark hung over the clutch.

Invading the world of motorcycling's jet set was a very pleasant experience but financially punishing and though I kept the MV for as long as possible I was nevertheless somewhat relieved when the appointed hour for its return arrived. I wanted to ride it all the time. That was the snag with this delightful machine. A journalist can't keep it in petrol.   V.W.

Test bike kindly loaned by Mike Ward of Wards Garage (Daybrook) of 835 Mansfield Road, Sherwood, Nottingham.

MV AGUSTA 750S AMERICA

Brilliant in red-and-silver, and traveling in a mushroom cloud of sound, the MV is far more than a stylish flash of light and noise.

● Nothing about the new MV Agusta 750S America is understated. Strong, visceral and bold, the bike overwhelms everything around it. This red-and-silver roadster becomes the indisputable center of attraction everywhere it deigns to appear. And the 750S America is overwhelming in other ways: it makes a conservative 75 horsepower, rushes through the standing quarter-mile in 13.06 seconds, passes the dragstrip timing lights at 105.14 mph, pulls like a truck from 2000 rpm, tips the decibel meter to 94 db(A), pierces its surroundings with an electrifying roar at 9000 rpm, runs far beyond 130 mph in fifth gear, weighs a chunky 562 pounds wet – and costs a princely $6000. This cast-aluminum bank vault possesses a haughty aristocratic presence. Not vainglorious – the MV Agusta is just purely haughty.

Aristocratic or not, you ask – double-checking your wallet pocket – is the 750S America, or any motorcycle, worth $6000? The answer to that obvious question pivots on two considerations: first, the relative size of the pricetag as measured against an individual's resources; and second, one's expectations of what $6000 should buy in a motorcycle.

Machines such as the MV Agusta usually receive predictable reviews by the motorcycle press. Usually, hyper-expensive machines cause roadtesters to soar off into some loose jive-rapture about money/ego/motorcycles/ and the density of the paint. Or the opposite occurs. Testers screw on their hard noses, and push around comparisons like so many shiny pennies. Both approaches, flighty passion and penny-grinding comparisons, share at least one starting point: someone would buy a $6000 motorcycle on a $6000 motorcycle budget. But that assumption doesn't truck much with reality. People who buy $6000 motorcycles operate on grandiose motorcycle budgets, and they don't need passion as a justification. Equally peripheral to them are dollar-for-dollar comparisons which quickly reach a point of diminishing relevancy in the real world of mega-buck motorcycle budgets.

So how should you approach a $6000 motorcycle? Simple. It starts with some hard facts of life. Motorcycles are toys for grown-ups. Six-thousand dollar motorcycles are toys for wealthy grown-ups. Because almost every motorcycle in the United States is a toy, no motorcycle is

worth grievous, oppressive sacrifices to own. If you had to mortgage your grandmother's silverware, or anything else, to buy an MV, it isn't worth it. Most roadtesters (and readers) couldn't write a check for an MV without flinching, but the Rich of Motor Culture are different. They can. So first and foremost, MV Agustas are for those who can afford them – painlessly – and who agree with MV's interpretation of what a $6000 motorcycle should be.

No matter how expensive, any motorcycle makes a series of trade-offs, such as speed for noise, or weight for convenience. No ultimate be-all/end-all machine exists for $6000 or any other price. If you want a silent motorcycle that weighs under 500 pounds, winks back at you with eight warning lights and has built-in stereo, then regardless of your resources, buying a 750S America would be a dreadful waste of money – and a perfectly splendid MV Agusta.

The 750S America is powerful, quick-stopping, stylish, comfortable, fuss-free, and loud. It's also quite heavy through it feels agile at legal speeds. The motorcycle handles well at normal paces, but it lacks outstanding handling at more energetic rates.

The things which the MV single-seater does best are the most easily perceived: appearance, acceleration, sound and speed. Everything has the look and feel of expensive quality, including the sand-cast dohc engine, the hand-hammered aluminum cold-air box, the suede saddle, hand and foot controls, and heavily chromed nuts and bolts. The MV engine, a magnificent piece of hardware, dominates the entire motorcycle. The four-cylinder engine appears massive and brutal; but close-up, the individual components have an intricate, almost delicate character.

Belying its considerable weight, the 750S America makes a tight, compact package. The steel tank and seat have the same spare lines of MV's current Grand Prix bikes. Its styling gives the machine a light, economical grace; nothing looks contrived or affected. The new roadster escaped the trendy angular styling of Giorgetto Giugiaro and his rectilinear pencil.

The sensual MV broadcasts the best sound trip in motorcycling. Through the dragstrip traps, things sound as if there's a Grand Prix war in full progress. When the MV double-knocker peaks at 9000 rpm, you understand what the British press means by that quaint trans-atlanticism "full chat".

The 750S America represents the kind of machine which MV Agusta and Commerce Overseas Corporation believe an affluent American clientele will buy for $6000. To anyone who knows anything about motorcycle Grand Prix racing, MV Agusta is a self-explanatory concept. Commerce Overseas Corporation in New York, long associated with MV Agusta in the helicopter business, is the sole United States importer for MV motorcycles. Chris Garville from COC and Jim Cotherman, an MV retailer in the United States with credentials as a racer-tuner-developer, went to the MV factory in the fall of 1974. The American duo proposed a series of changes to update the existing 750 MV Agusta. The factory took their proposals under advisement and began work on a revamped roadster. Garville and Cotherman, working in concert with factory personnel, saw the new motorcycle, embodying their suggestions, literally take shape. Contrary to the stereotyped Italian scenario, where tomorrow is always next year, the American project went forward rapidly. Inside fifty days, the

MV factory had a prototype rolling. The America project received important encouragement and support from Fredmano Spairani, an MV director. (Italophiles may remember Spairani as the corporate head of Ducati, when the Vee-twins were launched and the 750 Desmos won the inaugural Imola 200).

Power was a key consideration. The MV four-cylinder responded well to prodding because it contained all the basic ingredients for great performance. Fundamentally, the engine is the old 500 Grand Prix unit which MV raced successfully from the 1950s to the mid-1960s. When it first appeared in production form, the engine displaced 600ccs; later MV bumped it to 743cc, and now, in the America model, the capacity has gone to 788cc.

Its growth has been carefully monitored and controlled. MV does not work on the American hot-rod principle, "hog it out and hope for the best". MV precisely calculated the loads on all power-train components to guarantee reliability. And it paid off. At the dragstrip the MV's horsepower, weight and tall first gear savagely abused the clutch, which withstood the brutality without slipping or protesting or even serving notice.

Some of the power increase has come from enlarging the pistons two millimeters (bore and stroke are now 67mm x 56mm); another increment was added by raising the compression ratio (from 10:1 to 10.2:1), but the greatest power gain lies in the cylinderhead.

The cylinderhead has been recalibrated to deal with the increased displacement. The factory resisted the simple expedient of adding squish bands in the combustion chambers in order to cover the larger pistons. MV reflowed intake tracts, installed larger intake and exhaust valves, and completely resphered the combustion chambers.

Gone are the 24mm UBF Deli 'Orto carburetors which fed the first 750 Sports. In their stead are a quartet of 26mm VHP Dell 'Ortos which, unlike the old set-up, have completely enclosed tops. The old derrick slide-lifters are gone; the new MV has a single-cable race-type actuation mechanism.

While the 788 engine uses more carburetion than early 750s, the big engine actually has a milder camshaft, in terms of lift and duration. The immensely tractable engine has power from 2000 rpm to

9000 rpm.

Machinery fascinates nearly all motorcyclists; some find whirring gears and shafts positively addictive. Hardware junkies blow themselves away on MV engines. It is a masterpiece of precision castings, gears, needle bearings, ball bearings, shafts, and all other things in the hard goods department. Were it mass-produced, the engine would still be murderously expensive to build.

Item: A matched set of three straightcut gears runs up between the interior cylinders; this gear train, driven off the crankshaft, in turn drives the gears which turn the camshafts.

Item: The pressed-together crankshaft turns on ball bearings (at each end) and four enormous split-cage roller bearings at interior points. Unlike any other production engine in motorcycling, the crankshaft is held inside a separate cylinder-block casting, and this sub-assembly bolts into the main engine casting. This method of construction, a carry-over from MV racing engine design, gives the crankshaft incredibly strong support, minimizes thermal distortions, and eliminates the need for more complex and intricate casting/machining operations in a limited production engine.

Item: Because the Bosch dynastart generator lies behind the engine sump, the main engine cases are narrower than the cases of a CB-400 Honda.

An itemized catalogue of the MV engine's lovely, arcane, sophisticated hardware might stretch on for twenty pages. But the listing would be a cruel joke if this elaborate machinery only excelled at being elaborate. Or made no power. Or was fragile as brittle china.

The MV engine is rugged. It has that same run-on/run-on quality found in R90s BMWs and Honda 750s. There's every reason to believe that MV engines are set-it-and-forget-it propositions. After initial break-in (600 miles), the valve clearances can be set (.010 and .012), and experience has shown that the valves will not normally require further adjustment for about 10,000 miles. The Bosch distributor-type ignition is very automotive as is the Bosch starter/generator, and the drive-shaft eliminates any fussing with a chain. Basic service intervals come round every 3600 miles. The engine isn't temperamental. Our test bike would eventually wet-foul plugs because the carburetors had slides which produced extraordinarily rich mixtures. Re-sliding for local conditions would have leaned out the mixture to normal.

Italian machines traditionally have been spotted with ratty-tatty detailing. Not so with the MV 750S America. Italophiles will scarcely believe it, but Aprilia has finally built real handlebar switches with cast aluminum bodies and plastic buttons. The switches follow the same pattern as Yamaha controls. The 750 America shifts on the left side, and brakes on the right. The switch has been done neatly inside the engine cases, so no Johnson-rod maze spoils the exterior. And at last MV Agustas have real air-filtration. A beautiful hand-hammered aluminum cold-air-box houses a very simple dry synthetic filter.

The running gear changes have likewise been extensive between the old 750S and the America model. When Cycle last encountered the MV 750 Sport, the bike had a four-shoe front brake. That anchor has been replaced by double discs with Scarab calipers and master cylinder. Our test MV has the best Scarab disc brake system which we've tried; for feel and accuracy it's almost in the same league as Lockheed components. The America model has a massive Ceriani fork which replaces less formidable models on earlier MVs. The heavy-duty Ceriani has 38mm tubes and wider, stronger triple clamps than previous equipment. The frame, which retains the same 55-inch wheelbase and basic geometry, has a longer, stronger steering neck.

MV made no changes in the driveshaft unit nor in the gear ratios — primary, transmission, and final. The swing arm has been taken straight off old models, as have the Sebac rear dampers.

Our test America, which was literally the first production bike built, varied from later bikes in three ways. First, the instrument panel, à la Ducati, has been scrapped in favor of the alloy instrument holders fitted to previous 650 Sport models. This substitution brings the ignition switch back between the instruments. Furthermore, gas taps will be activated by the ignition switch, as per Moto Guzzi, and the centerstand tow-down bar, which ground slightly, will be raised a bit.

Space relationships have been thoughtfully worked out on the MV 750S America. Since the MV's suede saddle is firm, the roadster's comfort grows out of the relative positioning of pegs, bars and seat. Not only is the saddle just 29 inches off the ground, it's relatively low to the clip-ons — which have built-in risers. Moreover, the tank isn't excessively long. The foot pegs have been positioned low enough so that the rider's knees aren't tucked into his armpits. The foot controls intersect nicely with hands and feet; no awkward groping is necessary. The controls operate with a velvet softness, and the engine contributes to the luxurious placidity. The engine vibrated less than a CB-750 but perhaps a bit more than a CB-550.

Of course, the America can't match the BMW R90S for sheer luxurious comfort. The MV is more restful than other genuine clip-on roadsters, namely the John Player Norton, the Ducati Sport and Super Sport, or the Laverda SFC. Although the saddle has far less padding than a Moto Guzzi Sport, a 265-mile jaunt revealed no great difference in riding fatigue between the MV and Guzzi.

The Bosch starter-generator spins the engine silently. With no preliminaries, the Italian four-cylinder whoofs into action, creating a mushroom cloud of sound: gear-meshing noise from the cylinder head chest balanced by the angry snarls from the four mufflers. Nicking the throttle skyrockets the tach-needle and curls your ears. The engine has no flywheel inertia, so instant throttle response is the engine's middle name.

With the standard exhaust system the rider can't escape the noise. Most enthusiasts wouldn't want to snuff out those intoxicating sounds. However, MV does manufacture a special exhaust system for the America, and the new plumbing, together with a fairing, will back off the volume to 84 db (A). Cycle staffers sampled the decibels-down mufflers for a half-hour, and then reverted to the more standard-music mufflers.

Without question, the 750S America joins that small (and dwindling) coterie of high performance street motorcycles. The driveshaft prevented any dynamometer testing; nevertheless, the dragstrip testing confirmed its strength. Bearing in mind its quarter-mile handicaps (weight 60-mph first gear, 140 mph fifth gear), the MV snapped through in 13.06 with a terminal velocity of 105.14. That's really impressive since the MV gives away lots of time in the first 150 feet. Lighter motorcy-cles with larger engines geared more appropriately for the dragstrip (Laverda 1000 and Kawasaki Z-1B) will stop the clocks quicker and deliver slightly higher trap speeds (Laverda 1000, 12.95 @ 106.13, Kawasaki Z-1B, 12.37 @ 107.36). But no matter what you own, don't bother trying to outrun the 750S America on the top end. At 85 mph (where it just has cleared second gear), the MV's close-ratio gearbox and compact size works to its advantage. The 750S America would slip away from Cycle Magazine's favourite Z1-B (dyno-tested at 83 horsepower) from 80 mph upwards. Though no suitable place exists to test for meaningless top speed figures, our test bike was easily strong enough to climb well into the 130s.

On board the MV certainly sounds brutish, but no harshness feeds into the controls. The clutch lever has a soft draw and a wide, predictable engagement arc. The gearbox shifts with the accuracy and feel of a bolt-action rifle. When the throw of the left-side shifter pedal was tightened up, it duplicated the touch and feel of right-side shifting MVs, which do the best gear-changes of all street roadsters. The twistgrip has a soft return spring, burning off a long-time Italian wart.

You needn't be Superman to make the front tire moan. The powerful dual discs system has no sponginess in it. Braking force goes up in a nice linear way, without demanding excessive muscle. By comparison, the rear drum brake doesn't exist. It feels almost powerless, and there's not much feedback. It's the single control distinguished by vagueness and fuzziness.

The heavy duty front discs are absolutely imperative, considering the MV's 562-pound wet weight and the speeds at which the engine will propel this mass. The MV outweighs the only other bikes of similar size and power. The Laverda 1000 pushes the scales to 520 pounds, down 40 on the MV: Kawasaki's Z-1B comes in at 540 pounds, undercutting the MV by 20 pounds. Other driveshaft motorcycles, the BMW R90S and Moto Guzzi Sport, are substantially lighter than the MV—70 pounds. The America's compactness can fool you; it looks much lighter than it is. Pulling the bike on its centerstand (without knowing the trick) at once suggests how heavy the MV is. Surprisingly, all the weight isn't in the engine. The complete unit, including starter-generator and carburetors, weighs just over 200 pounds. The MV carries a great deal of unsprung weight, especially at the rear, thanks to the driveshaft system.

The choice of tires, tire combinations (in terms of front-to-back match) and rim widths make an astonishing difference in cornering power (and the feel of that power) on any motorcycle. A so-called perfect combination for a given machine may only evolve after an extended period of trial and error. For some machines, it never happens. With a bike as heavy and powerful as the MV, the choice and balance is critical. Our test bike came equipped with a Metzeler 3.50 x 18 Rille rib on the front rim (2.16 inches bead-head width) and a 4.00 x 18 Metzeler C7 racing-clock pattern on the rear trim (2.5 inches). With the front inflated to 28 psi and the rear 32 psi (cold readings), the MV would weave and snake treacherously in fast corners. At those pressures, the handling produced bone-chilling fright in the rider. Leaving the front tire alone and lowering the cold pressure in the rear tire to 26 psi produced a stable condition without causing tire overheating. Hot pressure in the rear tire checked out at 30 psi.

Moderately hard cornering was then perfect on smooth bends, but a bump in a fast corner used up the rear suspension movement (even with full spring preload on the shocks) and a slow oscillation would result. The MV drifts through corners more than most motorcycles, especially lighter bikes. A slow, controlled drift without oscillation means that a bike is able to use all the available tire adhesion without causing the frame to flex resonantly. With the MV, there's an awful lot of weight on the front wheel and much more development time needs to be spent on tire and wheel selection, as well as shock absorbers, for racing-speed conditions.

The MV doesn't handle as well as a Laverda 1000. Compared to a competently prepared Kawasaki Z-1, the MV is taut and stable when the tires are inflated properly. The Z-1 mushes around and cushes against its cornering limit. The MV approaches its boundary more directly and without a lot of preliminary wiggles and loose-jointedness. And at the limit the MV will corner at higher speeds without oscillation than the Z-1.

Alternate S & W shock absorbers

with stronger damping and heavier springs helped to control the MV's wobble-reaction in bumps through fast corners. But this stiffened the boulevard ride into harshness. Anyone who wants to push his MV 750S to its limit should be prepared to experiment with tires, rims and shock absorbers — and he should be an accomplished, experienced rider because the MV, unlike the Laverda 1000 (but like the Z-1), is neither easy nor comfortable to ride really hard.

Handling in terms of steering-response feel is slow and heavy. The MV can move you at such a blinding pace that the lack of flickery is reassuring. Decided and purposeful pressure must be applied to the appropriate handlebar, footrest and tank side in order to change the MV's attitude at great speed. The most advantageous rider position from which to guide the MV's path is a crouch in a constant upright stance without body lean relative to the bike. It is difficult to change one's body pressures accurately on a machine while hanging off to the pavement side.

Six-thousand dollar motorcycles don't qualify as disposable, throwaway items. So natural restraint and John Law, if nothing else, will keep MV riders away from hot-lick riding. At ordinary speeds, the MV does handle well enough, and produces no

disconcerting quirks across bumps in smooth roads. The short wheel-base and small amount of trail minimize the sense of weight. Compared to a Moto Guzzi Sport, the America responds more quickly to inputs at moderate speeds, though it's 70 pounds heavier than the Guzzi. Furthermore, there's a tremendous horsepower differential.

Again and again the MV impresses a rider with its style, smoothness, comfort and — most of all — its sheer power, which is accompanied by the ever-present MV music. The 750S America is a grand boulevardier suitable to street parading, mountain-road stroking, and autostrada smoking. Name any venue, the red-and-silver MV will be the star attraction.

Exclusivity comes at no extra cost. At the very best, MV can build 200 America models in 1975, all of which will land in the United States. With this limited production motorcycle MV has finally made a commitment to the American market. It's almost ironic. At the same time MV at last arrives, other high-performance European models are disappearing from the American scene. Moto Guzzi's American efforts have been totally concentrated on the 850 T. Farewell, 750 Guzzi Sport. At least for 1975, and perhaps longer, Ducati Sports and Super Sports Desmos cannot be imported into the United States. Both bikes are victims of right-hand shift legislation. And the factory, which can sell the entire production in Europe, sees no compelling reason to make a U.S. version. Also the newest Laverda we've seen still has right-hand shift; until that can be changed, you won't see Laverda 1000s here either. The BMW R90S, measured by Laverda-Ducati-MV standards, is a high-volume motorcycle, and fortunately the German twin won't disappear. But a distressing fact remains, those who like European interpretations of high-performance motorcycles may find their choices severely limited, or the options increasingly expensive.

Given those realities, every MV America 750 which lands in the United States will be snatched up. An eager welcome may encourage MV to build even more sporting motorcycles in the future. MV Agusta has financial, technical and manufacturing resources to offer a continuing line of high performance limited-production motorcycles. Exciting as the 750S America is today, we can hardly wait till tomorrow.

MV AGUSTA 750S AMERICA

Price, suggested retail	POE, New York, $6000
Tire, front	3.50 x 18 Metzeler Rille 10 Rib
rear	4.00 x 18 Metzeler Block C7 Racing Profile
Brake, front	11 in. x 1.4 in. x 2 (280mm x 35mm x 2)
rear	7.9 in. x 1.8 in. (200mm x 45mm)
Brake swept area	213.4 sq. in. (1376.4 cm²)
Specific brake loading	3.46 lbs./sq. in.
Engine type	Four-stroke dohc four
Bore and stroke	67mm x 56mm (2.638 in. x 2.205 in.)
Piston displacement	788 cm³ (48.08 cu. in.)
Compression ratio	10.2:1
Carburetion	4; 26mm VHB Dell'Orto
Air filtration	Dry synthetic fiber
Ignition	Battery and coil
Bhp @ rpm	NA
Torque @ rpm	NA
Rake/Trail	27°/3.2 in.
Mph/1000 rpm, top gear	15.3
Fuel capacity	5.0 gal. (19 liters)
Oil capacity	5.0 qt. (4.7 liters)
Electrical power	135 watts
Battery	12V, 14AH
Gear ratios, overall	(1) 11.68 (2) 8.45 (3) 6.47 (4) 5.44 (5) 4.98
Wheelbase	55 in. (139.7 cm)
Seat height	29 in. (73.6 cm)
Ground clearance	5.3 in. (13.4 cm)
Curb weight	562 lbs. (252.9 kg)
Test weight	740 lbs. (335.7 kg)
Instruments	Speedometer, odometer, tachometer
Standing start ¼-mile	13.06 sec.; 105.14 mph
Average fuel consumption	42.2 mpg
Speedometer error	30 mph, actual 26.52 60 mph, actual 54.36

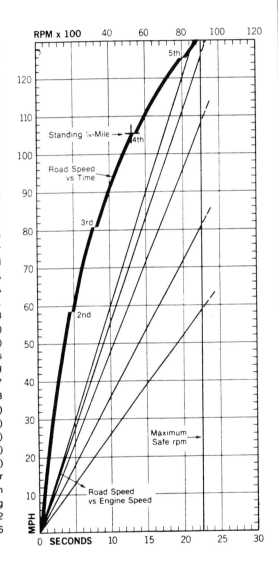

OWNER'S VIEW

With the knowledge that in all probability there are less than one hundred 750S America models in Britain, I had expected some difficulty in tracing owners who would agree to being interviewed. So I am more than grateful to members of the MV Agusta Owners Club who came to the rescue and provided all the background information I needed.

As may be expected in the case of such a elite machine, most riders purchased an MV four because of the marque's racing successes, having followed the fortunes of Surtees, Hailwood and Agostini on the race tracks of the world. To have a road-going version of the factory racers appealed greatly, the more so because it represented the very best in Italian engineering, had outstanding performance, and made a beautiful noise. Mature riders in the main, to them price was only a secondary consideration. To own an MV four was ego-boosting and to most there was a compelling urge to purchase one and indulge in the sheer pride of ownership. The fact that the machine represented an appreciating asset too, presented a bonus.

Dave Kay, the present Secretary of the MV Agusta Owners Club, is fortunate enough to own 4 MV fours – all of them Americas or their derivatives. So he was undoubtedly well-qualified to open my series of interviews:

JRC: Why are you so interested in the MV 750 America?
DK: I followed over the years the racing successes of MV, yet when in the late sixties an MV road bike was announced, I was a little disappointed. The 600 four had very angular lines, was dumpy and overweight, and had high rise handlebars, crash bars and a horrible rectangular headlamp. To me it was not an MV at all. Time passed, and when the 750S model was announced in all its glory I knew I would have to have one. But at the time my finances were severely restricted and as time progressed the chances of purchasing one seemed more and more remote. The crunch came when I read a road test report on the 750S America in an issue of Motor Cycle Weekly published during 1977. I must have read that report a dozen times, coupled with the fact that the factory was about to cease production. I decided that no matter what the consequences were, I just had to buy one.
JRC: When did you buy your machine?
DK: The machine was purchased second-hand from a Lincoln motor dealer for a sum that was at that time considered to be very expensive. The machine had done 2000 miles and I collected it during late 1977.
JRC: What condition was it in? Were some of the faults found common for this model?
DK: The condition of the cycle parts was as new. But from the onset trouble was experienced in starting the machine, due to a flat battery. A bump start brought the engine to life, sounding like a late 19th century agricultural vehicle. I was informed this was quite normal and that I would get used to it. After only two miles the engine cut out on two cylinders, caused by a nearly empty petrol tank, which a refill soon put right. After 20 miles or so the engine began to perform as it should. It no longer sounded like an antique tractor, the working tolerances of the engine now being correct. It performed according to expectations and sounded great. When I arrived home I realised that I had experienced my most memorable ride on a motorcycle.

JRC: What repair and general renovation work has been carried out?
DK: The quality of the chromium plating was poor and being of Italian origin, the switchgear and electrics were not up to the by now generally-accepted Japanese standards, being decidedly awkward to operate. These faults were apparent to the unbiassed eye. Repairs have been surprisingly few. The ignition and cam timings were checked and adjusted, both being slightly incorrect. Having an engine designed for 100 octane fuel, ignition advance is critical. If the setting is too far advanced, overheating and holed pistons will result. Even with the ignition timing set correctly, the engine runs at a high temperature – approximately 210-220°F oil temperature and 400°F at the cylinder head. Incorrect ignition timing can add another 10-20°F for every 2° advance.

The only other work required on the engine has been balancing the carburetters at regular intervals and shimming the exhaust valve clearances by inserting shims of the correct sizes between the valve stem ends and the inverted bucket cam followers. Rear tyres last approximately 3000 miles and front tyres 6000 miles. No basic troubles have been experienced with the America in 11,000 miles. However, I would recommend that any prospective purchaser of an MV buys a known example, as there are machines on the road which have been repaired by various "MV specialists" which have had problems in the engine department due to incorrect assembly.
JRC: Have you experienced any

problems in obtaining parts? If so, how were these problems overcome?

DK: Up to this point in time, no problems have been encountered. Spares were originally available from the concessionaires and these can now be obtained through the MV Agusta Owners Club as the club purchased all their spares when the link with the factory ended. The club now has close contact with the factory and all available spares can be obtained through this channel. If parts are ordered from Italy, usually they take an average of two months to be delivered, from the date of receipt of the order.

JRC: How does the machine perform and handle?

DK: In my opinion the four-cylinder MV engine is beyond criticism. It is over-engineered and is likely to suffer only as a result of crash damage. The only real problem lies in the gearbox, which is splash lubricated. Being remote, the layshaft outer bearing tends to break up after severe loadings have been imposed.

Handling is on a par with any other Italian machine that weighs 560lb, and due to its weight and the effects of the shaft final drive, it is not 'flickable' through corners. Physical effort is required through 'S' bends but this type of steering is soon assimilated by the rider. Some machines have a tendency to weave at around 90-100mph, usually on long, sweeping bends. In most cases this can be attributed to incorrect tyre pressures and incorrect adjustment of the swinging arm.

JRC: Do you use the machine regularly? Is this practical and if so, how do running costs work out?

DK: My machine is used for pleasure riding. It copes with town traffic reasonably well, but in traffic jams the engine tends to overheat, as does the clutch. I would have thought that for everyday use, this machine does not present a practical proposition. The cost of spares is on a par with those of Ducati and in nearly all cases they prove cheaper than their Japanese equivalents.

With a machine of this type I never attempt to calculate running costs; the machine is used solely for pleasure and the pleasure it gives is beyond price.

JRC: Has your machine won prizes in any events?

DK: One of the four machines I own, a 750 Sport that was imported into England, won the MV Agusta Concours prize at the 1982 Cadwell Park track meeting.

JRC: To what extent has club membership proved helpful?

DK: Club membership has proved helpful in that MV owners are spread thinly throughout the country, so that the track meetings held by the club tend to bring the more keen types together so that notes can be compared and problems discussed. The club magazine permits members to seek advice over running problems, to advertise machines for sale, and generally to compare views. By far the biggest advantage of membership is that the only spares available in Britain are obtainable through the club.

JRC: Is there an MV specialist you have found particularly helpful?

DK: Since owning an MV I have always serviced my machines personally as I have not found a garage or specialist I can trust with a machine of this quality. Most of the club members who ride MVs

have sufficient experience with other machines to carry out most tasks without problems. The factory manual is very explicit and easy to follow. Sadly, probably half the MVs in Britain have been purchased as investments and are not ridden. They are owned by persons with little or no practical motorcycling experience; maintenance is therefore not required.

For major rebuilds within the Birmingham area I acknowledge the work of Mark Wellings who, in my opinion, has destroyed more MV engines than anyone I know through hard riding. In so doing, he has acquired the practical experience to rebuild engine units to 'as new' condition.

JRC: How would you sum up the enjoyment you get from owning an MV America?

DK: To sum this up is difficult, as owning an MV represents a love/hate relationship. A flat battery, or some simple electrical fault, can make the engine refuse to start. After losing nearly a stone in weight trying to bump start a machine weighing nearly 600lb you wonder whether a Japanese machine would not provide a more viable alternative. But when the engine starts and the first three or four miles have passed, a feeling of total exhilaration takes over. Just listening to that exhaust note makes you a Surtees, Hailwood or Agostini as you swing into the bends. When those who have criticised an MV are offered a ride, the expression on their face says it all when they return. Inevitably they say that never was a ride enjoyed more.

JRC: What advice would you give to a potential owner of an MV America?

DK: The only advice I can give is that they join the MV Agusta Owners Club. I may be biassed as I am Secretary of the club, but club members do sell their machines from time to time, and all the MV fours in the club have a known history.

Although Dave had tried to give an impartial answer to my questions, it was only to be expected that he would be much in favour of the club which takes so much of his spare time. Yet the reasons for becoming a member seen sound enough, if only to bond the enthusiastic riders together and keep them separate from the speculators who regard an MV four much as an art collector would regard a Renoir or a Picasso. Mention has been made already of Mark Wellings, renowned for his hard riding. So it was his comments I sought next:

JRC: Why are you interested in the MV 750 America?
MW: MV Agusta are the only manufacturer who learned how to build and design bikes on the race tracks of the world, before selling their products to customers. With each MV four you own a piece of racing history.
JRC: When and why did you buy your machine?
MW: The machine I have at present is the third MV four I have owned. I swapped an SB2 Bimota for it because I prefer MVs.
JRC: What condition was it in? Were some of the faults found common for this model?
MR: The paintwork needed attention, plus some general maintenance which was overdue. The steering head bearings were too tight, as was the swinging arm. The rear suspension units had to be changed for Konis. All these faults are common.
JRC: What repair and general renovation work has been carried out?
MW: The engine was completely rebuilt, using the opportunity to increase the capacity to 832cc. The parts fitted included special camshafts to increase performance, larger inlet and exhaust valves, a gas-flowed cylinder head, 30mm accelerator pump carburetters, straight-cut crankshaft pinions, and racing clutch linings. The frame was fitted with Spondon adjustable forks and Dymag wheels, and a

Moto Guzzi linked braking system added. No problems were encountered in obtaining spares as a result of MV Agusta Owners Club membership.
JRC: How does the machine perform and handle?
MW: Having owned many superbikes, including a Benelli 900, I find that in comparison the MV has the best handling of all, apart from the SB2 Bimota. Although it is not the quickest on acceleration, it has a top speed in excess of all.
JRC: Do you use your machine regularly? Is this practical, and if so, how do the running costs work out?
MW: I have twice travelled around Europe with my wife Irene as pillion passenger, so I have found it quite practical to use in this manner. Fuel consumption averages out at 40mpg at a speed of 80mph. Very little oil is consumed – about 11,500 miles per pint.
JRC: To what extent has club membership proved helpful, other than for spares, as mentioned earlier?
MW: I have met a lot of people who have one thing in common – a love of the MV four. Also I have picked up many interesting facts about MVs.
JRC: Is there an MV specialist you found particularly helpful?
MW: I have to date rebuilt five engines and have had no problems. I can contact Dave Kay who has

also worked on these machines and between us, I would doubt whether there is anything we do not know about the MV fours.
JRC: How would you sum up the enjoyment you get from owning an MV four?
MW: It has to be the best way to ride, every part of the machine oozing class and beauty. When you ride an MV Agusta you realise what the term 'The Power and the Glory' means, and there is the added bonus that your machine is appreciating in value. That in itself is cheap motorcycling – if you are ever stupid enough to sell your bike!
JRC: What advice would you give a potential owner of an MV America?
MW: Ride it!

As mentioned earlier, it is the more mature rider who is likely to be attracted to owning an MV four, often because past racing successes and a whole string of famous names can be associated with the days when they followed road racing and made the annual pilgrimage to the Isle of Man. Bill Hicks is just one of those splendid people who will continue to ride bikes as long as they can lift a leg over the saddle. Now in his 63rd year and wishing he were 20 years younger (though he is in heart), Bill's views were well worth seeking:

JRC: Why are you so interested in the MV 750S America?
BH: My interest started a long while ago, in the Isle of Man. I was there when Surtees, McIntyre, Agostini, Hailwood, Provini, etc, fought their epic battles, and I shall never forget the sound of those red ''Fire Engines''. I knew that if ever there was a chance, I would buy an MV four, but it seemed an impossible dream. I never thought I would have the privilege of owning a bike similar to that ridden by the late Mike Hailwood.

JRC: When and why did you buy your machine?

BH: I bought my present machine two years ago. Earlier, I had bought a brand new America, but I had to sell it for health reasons. But after a while the bug bit again and I just couldn't live without an MV. So I acquired a second-hand Monza. My reasons for buying an MV were because I was looking for something different, something with a pedigree a mile long and the sort of bike that few others would have. It also had to look good and go like hell! There's a very satisfying sense of one-upmanship about owning an MV.

JRC: What condition was it in? Were some of the faults found common for this model?

BH: The previous owner was an Italian, the machine having been seen in Italy, bought and shipped back to England, then advertised in *Motor Cycle News*. It was in good external condition and couldn't be faulted, but after a while I blew a piston and with the aid of the MV Agusta Owners Club I found the ignition timing and mixture settings were not as they should have been. It was then that I realized that everything has to be spot-on if the engine is to withstand a thrashing. This also applies as regards handling, in the case of tyres, suspension etc.

With regard to faults, I would agree with road testers that the clutch is the weak point, although only when I thrash the bike around Cadwell Park can I make it slip. The oil dipstick could be improved, also the quality of the switchgear, starter button etc. And if you ride two-up, the original equipment seat is not really suitable.

JRC: What repair and general renovation work has been carried out?

BH: As mentioned previously, repairs were necessary as a result of the blown piston. This necessitated setting the ignition timing and the mixture strength correctly after the engine rebuild. I have also had the seals renewed in the rear disc brake master cylinder and problems with a slipping starter belt, the latter solved by re-shimming. Acting on the advice of Dave Kay, a single contract beaker was fitted to the distributor in place of the twin points set-up fitted as original.

JRC: Have you experienced problems in obtaining parts? If so, how were these problems overcome.

BH: No problems really, because the parts I needed for my engine rebuild were readily available from the concessionaires. Since then, the club has acquired all these spares. On occasions a club member has visited Italy and has been able to bring back parts to order. Quite a number of items such as vee belts, cables etc can be purchased quite readily from most motorcycle agents.

JRC: How does the bike perform and handle?

BH: My machine handles and performs very much as the road test reports suggest. I've never had my machine up to maximum speed, although I did once work up to 135mph, which I found most exhilarating! MVs do wriggle a bit, but only when going pretty quickly around a sweeping bend. They will also weave when hitting potholes or when encountering a raised white line on a bend. All that is necessary is to shut off and continue on your chosen line, when all will be well. MVs are very forgiving. I've never had a moment's panic or felt I couldn't handle a given situation at any time. Even when I hit spilled diesel fuel, the bike came out as an MV should.

JRC: Do you use your bike regularly? Is this practical, and if so, how do running costs work out?

BH: I use my machine regularly during the warm, dry weather. As I'm now a bit old in the tooth, I no longer enjoy getting soaked just for the sake of it. The bike is not practical, however, for local shopping or even passing through cities. The engine gets very hot (especially with a fairing fitted) and the exhaust note frightens the odd cat and dog. Economy? I don't bother about that!

JRC: Has your machine won prizes in any events?

BH: No, but along with other club members I have ridden in many parades at race circuits and have received much heartfelt thanks from enthusiasts for giving them the privilege of hearing and inspecting these magnificent machines.

JRC: To what extent has club membership proved helpful?

BH: Club membership has undoubtedly proved very helpful indeed. Every MV owner ought to join, if only to get an idea of how many variants there are. Our meetings in pubs or at tracks have always proved to be an exciting and interesting highlight. There are some chaps who must know an MV engine nearly as well as Arturo Magni!

JRC: Is there an MV specialist you found particularly helpful?

BH: No, I can't think of one – apart from some of our club members.

JRC: How would you sum up the enjoyment you get from owning an MV Agusta?

BH: The very fact of owning an MV four, let alone riding the same "beast" Agostini rode is really something. Wherever one stops, a crowd is sure to gather and the police stop us regularly 'just to have a look, Sir'. To me, it is the ultimate for sheer riding fun and thrills. There are many other bikes that cost half as much, which are just as quick and eyecatching as the MV, but it is not quite the same – it's like comparing a Ford, as good as they undoubtedly are, to a Rolls-Royce. In four words – they're great, it's magic.

JRC: What advice would you give to a potential owner of an MV Agusta?

BH: I would think it would be essential to have owned a number of machines of this type, in order to appreciate the different characteristics. Owners would need to have a good mechanical knowledge as most MV owners prefer to do their own timing and maintenance. A first-time owner should understand that if he drops his machine, the repair work could prove very expensive. Finally, he should appreciate that if he is contemplating long distance touring, two-up and with panniers, an MV would be the last bike to buy. But if several machines are owned, and used for different purposes, I'll wager which one will give him the feeling that he has really lived, when he comes back from a ride!

Much of what Bill said has been echoed by two other MV Agusta Owners Club members, so that one begins to see the common bond that unites this small but very exclusive club. Bill Johnson has been an MV fanatic since 1960, having acquired his first MV (a 125) at the age of 16. When the 750S America became available, he bought one of the first to arrive in Britain. A motorcycle mechanic by trade, he acknowledges that all the faults found on his machine were common to the Americas in general. The most serious is the clutch, which he considers too small to handle the power output. Obtaining parts has presented no problems (through club membership) and he has found the machine comes into its own around 90-100mph out in the country. Town use is out and he uses his machine during the summer months only. Just to be MV owner is a reward in itself.

Peter Eacott bought an America in 1977, after talking to someone who road tested bikes for a magazine. His praise for the MV was sufficient to win Peter over. All that has required attention on his machine has been the Smiths tachometer and the need to get the plated parts re-chromed. Replacement parts have been limited to a new tachometer drive cable and an exhaust pipe locknut. He too is glad the club have assumed responsibility for spares and he hopes they will be in a position to have parts made when the remaining factory spares are used up.

Performance, and in particular handling, he considers can be enhanced by fitting better tyres, rear suspension units and other items that become expendable. Club membership is considered essential, to take advantage of a unique situation in which members are more than willing to help each other whenever possible. This is all the more important now that there is no longer an MV specialist in Britain.

Summing up, Peter believes that owning an MV four is simply ego-boosting and that the potential buyer should purchase one as soon as he can because it is something he will never regret.

From all this, one significant fact seems to emerge. As far as possible, the potential purchaser should obtain the best machine he can get for his money. The fours are built to racing standards and assembled with great care and precision. To obtain one that requires attention can result in very heavy expenditure to put it right, even if the initial purchase price is low. More to the point, it would seem that there are very few who can be trusted to undertake a complete rebuild to an acceptable standard, One has only to refer to a case history under the heading 'Requiem for an MV' in the Spring 1982 issue of *MV News* to understand just how serious a problem this can be. The post-mortem on the £1100 rebuild makes interesting reading, the more so because it took both hands on the crankshaft faces to make it rotate, after the crankshaft, complete with carriers and pistons, had been transferred to the workbench!

BUYING

Two immediate problems will confront the prospective purchaser of one of these machines – the small number that come up for sale each year and, when a machine is finally located, being able to check on its past history so that something about its mechanical history is known. Most of those who own 750S America models seem determined to keep them, a few owners regarding them basically as an appreciating asset. With only 58 examples belonging to members of the MV Agusta Owners Club it could be inferred that with but a few exceptions, it is mainly the rougher examples that tend to change hands.

Even assessing the value of an America can prove difficult as undoubtedly some of the prices asked are of a speculative nature and not necessarily indicative of the going rate. Unfortunately, reference to *Glass's Guide* will not help, for although the MV fours are listed, the suggested buy-in values are something like $\frac{1}{8}$th of what one would expect to pay for a good example! Any good MV four does command a high price, as one would expect in the case of a machine that was made in very limited numbers and has an inpeccable pedigree. But this can be offset to some extent by the realisation that it is a machine that will continue to appreciate in value, provided it is well looked after and maintained in good running order. The true MV enthusiast uses his bike and takes great pride in doing so.

From the prospective purchaser's viewpoint, there is much to be gained in joining the MV Agusta Owners Club as a first move. As has been mentioned earlier, the history of machines belonging to club members is easily checked out, so that there is less chance of buying a machine of unknown quality. Perhaps more to the point, a machine can be expected to change hands at a realistic price. Relatively few machines come up for sale in either of the motorcycling weeklies, or the classic motorcycle magazines.

A few machines have been acquired from Italy, either by direct purchase or through one of the Italian machine specialists based in this country. It is alleged that machines come cheaper this way, although this is open to conjecture. In both cases shipping costs have to be met and also customs duties paid, to say nothing of all the paperwork that needs to be completed. On the one hand, much personal involvement will be required in order to complete the transaction, whilst on the other a mark-up on the purchase price can be expected to cover all additional expenses and overheads. In either case, the mechanical condition of the machine may still be an unknown quantity. From the initial start-up, any MV four will have a high level of mechanical noise until the working parts reach their optimum temperature and hence their correct tolerances. This can take upwards of 20 miles riding, to which the seller is unlikely to agree.

The question of whether there is an advantage in buying a cheap machine that needs a complete overhaul is hardly likely to arise, because it is difficult to see any advantage in adopting this approach. Quite apart from the difficulty of obtaining spares (other than through the MV Agusta Owners Club) there are very few specialists who could be relied upon to undertake work of this nature which, in any case, would prove very expensive. The MV fours were built to racing standards and as such, need to be set up correctly if they are to give good, reliable service. Even fewer motorcyclists would have sufficient skill and experience to undertake repair work of this nature themselves, discounting the need for adequate garage space and the necessary equipment.

Fortunately, renovation of the cycle parts would cause no undue problems, with so many facilities available today for bead blasting, enamelling and plating. Some components, such as tyres and rear suspension units, can often be replaced by equivalents of better quality which will help give the machine even better handling qualities; assuming there is no desire to keep to the manufacturer's original specification. It is all a question of what the owner wants, and expects, from his machine.

Sometimes an MV four comes up at an auction and it is here that the prospective owner may so easily get carried away in the heat of the moment. Commission can add substantially to the purchase price a machine of this nature can be expected to demand, and it is easy to overstep the mark when bidding against a rival. Here, more than anywhere else, the rule of *caveat emptor* applies. If you do intend to make a bid, take a good look at the machine during the viewing session that precedes the auction and if possible, check it out with someone who knows the MV fours quite well. If you are lucky, you may get a bargain, but you are unlikely to hear the engine run until the machine has become your property and it may then be too late.

The perfect motorcycle has yet to be made and whilst the MV fours come close to their owners' expectations, they have faults which seem to be common throughout the range. Foremost amongst these are the doubtful quality of the chromium plating and in some cases the paintwork, the generally poor quality of the electrical switchgear and its inconvenient layout, and a somewhat inadequate clutch that will only just handle the power output if maintained in first-class condition. Comments have been made about the tendency for the engine to become ''fussy'' and to overheat in dense traffic conditions, but this criticism may be a little unfair as a racing type engine, designed to run on 100 octane fuel and with very little flywheel inertia, can hardly be expected to double up in a satisfactory manner for commuter use. The bonus, of

course, lies in the performance of the machine and the fact that it is virtually an over-the-counter four cylinder racer. Inevitably a compromise has to be reached and it can be argued that MV got the balance just about right, bearing in mind that prospective purchasers would never see the machine fulfilling a commuter or touring role.

To sum up, buying any MV four is likely to be a gamble unless the machine's past history can be verified. As time progresses, the

machines currently in use are going to require more attention, which suggests that this factor will become one of increasing consideration against a background of ever rising values. There is much to be said for buying as soon as the right opportunity occurs.

790cc America	58
832cc Boxer	2
832cc Monza	10
862cc Monza Arturo	
Magni	5
1000cc Corona	2
	91

CLUBS, SPECIALISTS & BOOKS

Club

With such a small number of machines imported into Britain, it will be appreciated why there is only one club that caters specifically for owners of MV fours. This is the **MV Agusta Owners Club**, which has as its patrons Phil Read and John Surtees. The club issues a regular official newsletter to its members under the title *MV News* and was successful in acquiring all the MV spares when the UK concessionaire was forced to sever connections with the factory when the manufacture of motorcycles eventually ceased. Further information about the Club and its activities can be obtained from the present Secretary:

Dave Kay,
26, Lichfield Road,
Shire Oak,
Sandhills,
Nr. Walsall Wood,
Staffs, WS9 9PE, England.

Just for the record, the breakdown of the fours owned by MV Agusta Owners Club members is as follows:

600cc	3
743cc GT Sport	2
743cc Sport	8
790cc Super Sport	1

Books

Very little has been written about the MV fours on their own, apart from a book, a brief history of the marque in a serial work *(On Two Wheels)*, and a series of articles in *Motorcycle Sport*. The full references are as follows:

The Story of the MV Agusta Motor Cycles by Peter Carrick. Published by Patrick Stephens Ltd, 1979. 128 pages, many black and white illustrations.

Champion of Champions by Jeff Clew. Published by Orbis Publishing Ltd, 1979, in *On Two Wheels*, Issue No. 58.

MV Comes of Age by Roy Bacon. Published in *Motorcycle Sport*, Nov 1970-Sept 1971 (serialised article).

Foreign Racing Motorcycles by Roy Bacon. Published by Foulis/Haynes, 1979. Whilst this book is not solely about MVs, it does contain an abbreviated history of the marque's racing activities.

Specialists

Sadly, there is no longer an official MV repair specialist. However, it is interesting to note that Dave Kay is able to carry out repairs to club members' machines through a business trading as **MVA Motorcycles Ltd.** Here, facilities are available to carry out major overhauls to engine and cycle parts.

PHOTO
GALLERY

1

1. The first of the 743cc models was brought into
Britain during 1972, the basic model being designated
the 750GT. As can be seen, this model featured very
different styling from the models that were to follow –
but did have a purposeful attractiveness. Note the
somewhat amateur-looking model designation on the
side panel. (Motorcycle Sport)

2. This 750S model is fitted with the full fairing supplied by the factory. There can be no mistaking the name of the manufacturer!

3. The left-hand side of the 750S model. Note the cutaway in the lower silencer for the centre stand operating arm.

2

3

4. *The side panels of the 750S model are much smaller and of different shape to those fitted to the disc front brake models.*

5. *The impressive double sided front drum brake is of the twin leading shoe type and is ventilated to offset the risk of brake fade.*

6. *The other side of the twin front brake assembly. Note the lead wire wrapped around two of the wheel spokes to balance the wheel.*

4

5

6

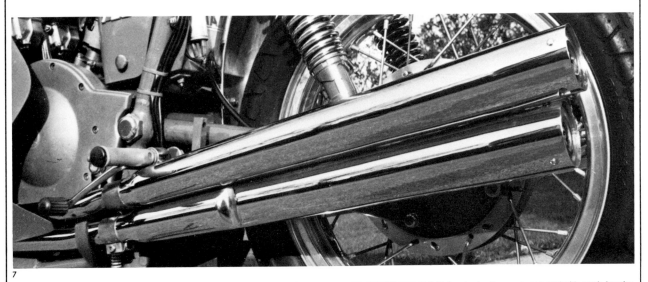

7

7. Quadruple silencers, two on each side, are in keeping with the racing heritage of the 750S. They almost completely obscure the large diameter rear drum brake.

8. The fairing helps accentuate the slim frontal view of the MV four and conveniently accommodates the large diameter and very effective headlamp.

8

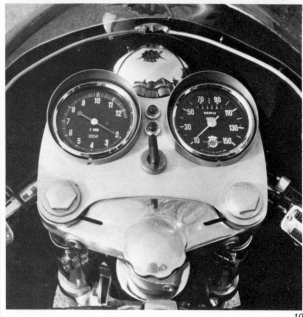

9. A distinctive feature of the 750S model is the petrol tank, finished in blue with a white flash.

10. This view of the "cockpit" shows the matching speedometer and tachometer mounted in their respective binnacles. In front of the ignition key is a generator warning light and the headlamp main beam indicator.

11. Not so apparent in the previous side view is the way in which the petrol tank is sculptured to give a particularly pleasing effect. Capacity is just over 5 gallons.

12

13

12. Final drive is by shaft, which runs through the right-hand tube of the swinging arm fork. The bevel housing is heavily finned to aid cooling.

13. This unfaired 750S model has twin front disc brakes and differently shaped side panels. There is no longer a cutaway in the lower of the two silencers for the centre stand operating arm.

14

15

14. The other side of the disc brake 750S model shows the small fairing and screen that surrounds the headlamp.

15. A close-up of the side panel fitted to the left-hand side of the disc brake 750S model.

16. It seems doubtful whether any other manufacturer has ever produced such a clean looking set of crankcase castings. Allen screws are used to good effect.

17. The four Dell'Orto carburetters have extended air intakes, without air cleaners. Synchronisation is aided by the adjustable "rockers" that operate the slides.

18. The cylinder head is a monobloc casting, whereas the cylinder barrels are cast individually. All castings are of undeniably high quality.

19. The double overhead camshafts are gear driven through a tunnel located between the middle cylinder barrels.

20. In this close-up of the engine unit the Bosch distributor can be seen, between the middle carburetters. The condenser is clipped to its side.

21

22

23

21. The rear light is of distinctive design and somewhat reminiscent of American practice.

22. The hinged seat is too short to be comfortable for both a rider and passenger. It is covered with a bright red coloured material.

23. This disc front brake 750S America model is probably an early example as the side panel does not carry the America name. (Motorcycle Sport)

24. This right-hand view of a 750 America model shows a number of changes in styling from the earlier 750S models, particularly with regard to the petrol tank, seat, side panels and front mudguard.

24

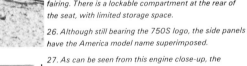

25. This machine too has the factory-supplied full fairing. There is a lockable compartment at the rear of the seat, with limited storage space.

26. Although still bearing the 750S logo, the side panels have the America model name superimposed.

27. As can be seen from this engine close-up, the America has a different type of Dell'Orto carburetter, to which is attached an air cleaner. A bank of four is still used.

28. The right-hand end of the handlebars showing the kill switch, horn button and hydraulic fluid reservoir for the front disc brake assembly. This example has been fitted with aircraft quality hoses.

29. Following racing practice, the handlebars have extended ends to take the brunt of any impact. The headlamp switchgear is not too convenient to operate with gloved hands.

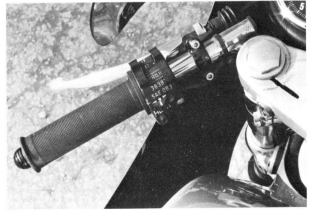

30

31

32

33

30. Although the America model has twin front discs, the rear brake is of the internal expanding shoe design.

31. In keeping with modern practice, the rider's footrests are of the folding variety and slim in profile. The gearchange pedal is conveniently to hand and has only a short adjustable operating rod.

32. The pillion passenger's footrests fold too, and are of virtually identical design. The shaft drive arrangement of the 750 America is identical in appearance and layout to that of the earlier models.

33. The distinctive and colourful MV Agusta logo.

34. The Brembo front disc brake assembly uses cast iron discs and is of the twin unit type. The speedometer drive is taken from the left-hand side of the wheel hub.

35. The seat of the America is covered in a black, non-slip material but is still not sufficiently comfortable for rider and passenger.

34

35

36

37

38

39

36. The "cockpit" layout of the America is even neater than that of the earlier 750S models, with an extended set of warning lights.

37. The rear internal expanding hub brake of the America is still almost completely obscured by the twin silencers on the left-hand side.

38. The view that riders of most other machines will see!

39. The 832cc Boxer model, a somewhat curious choice of name on account of the in-line four engine configuration. Later, this name was abandoned in favour of Monza, when the car manufacturers Ferrari objected to its use. They had prior right to the use of the name. (Motorcycle Sport)

40. The Monza model (832cc) is mainly identifiable by cosmetic modifications, like the different paint styling and the 'Monza' name on fairing and side panels.

40

41

42

43

41. Right-hand shot of the same bike. This example features gas-filled rear suspension units.

42. The Monza, like the Boxer before it, has disc brakes all round.

43. A close-up of the Monza's twin front discs: drilled to improve efficiency, particularly in the wet. The examples shown are of Brembo manufacture. Now spoked alloy wheels are in use too.

44. A glimpse of the Monza engine almost completely obscured by the fairing, however the choke lever on the outer carburetter is readily visible.

45. Monza "cockpit" balance is upset by having the tachometer with a face that no longer matches that of the speedometer.

44

45

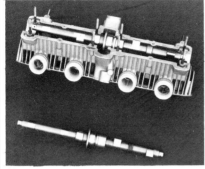

46

47

50

46. The cylinder head casting with one camshaft removed. Note the skew gear from which the drive to the tachometer is taken.

47. Another view of the cylinder head casting, with both camshafts removed. Note the "peaky" profile of the cams.

48

49

48. The four separate cylinder barrels showing the domed pistons and one-piece connecting rods with reinforced big end eyes.

49. The multi-plate clutch assembly which some consider is only just adequate for the power output of the engine.

50. The gearbox end cover on the left is for the conventional shaft final drive, and that on the right for chain final drive.

51

52

51. The early MV fours had their handling problems, which Les Graham did much to ease. This photograph, almost certainly taken during the first lap of the 1953 Senior TT, shows Les airborne and about to make a tricky front wheel landing. Sadly, he was killed during the second lap of this race when he crashed at the foot of Bray Hill. (National Motor Museum)

52. By the time John Surtees joined MV the fours were really coming into their own, and presenting a formidable challenge. This photograph was taken during the 1956 Senior TT, which John won at an average speed of 96.57mph. (National Motor Museum)

53

54

55

56

53. John Hartle was another English rider who rode the MV fours with some success. Here he is seen on the 350cc four during the 1960 Junior TT, which he won at an average speed of 96.70mph. (National Motor Museum)

54. Rhodesian Gary Hocking took the 1961 and 1962 500cc World Championship titles for MV under the guise of a private entrant. Taken during the 1962 Senior TT race, this photograph does not show the farcical 'MV Privat' label that would have been stuck on the fuel tank. He won at an average speed of 103.51mph. (National Motor Museum)

55. Indisputably the greatest of them all, Mike Hailwood joined MV at the end of the 1961 racing season, and remained with the company for four very eventful years. He made sure MV retained their 500cc World Championship throughout this period and is seen here on his way to victory in the 1964 Senior TT, which he

won at an average speed of 100.95mph. (National Motor Museum)

56. Another legendary name associated with MV is that of Giacomo Agostini, who enjoyed as large a following in Britain as in his native Italy. This photograph, taken at Quarter Bridge during the 1968 Junior TT, shows Agostini sweeping past Tom Dickie (350cc Petty Norton). He went on to win at an average speed of 104.78mph. (National Motor Museum)

C1A

C1B

C1A & C1B. The factory-made fairing on this drum-braked 750S provides the welcome touch of a white relief whilst the logo leaves no doubt about the machine's manufacturer!

C2

C3

C2. It would be interesting to know why, on the 750S models, the petrol tank was finished in blue with a white flash, whereas the rest of the machine was in red? Fortunately, the overall effect is pleasing.

C3. Not apparent from a side view, the 750S petrol tank has a red painted top, relieved only by the MV logo and a thin white line. This is the closest that most of us will get to sitting astride an MV!

C4

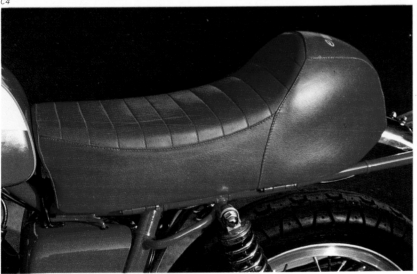

C5

C4. The petrol tank has a specially-sculptured shape, being broader at the bottom. Note the unusual arrangement of the transfer wording on the right-hand side.

C5. The 750S models, both disc and drum braked, have the dual seat covered in red material. Although the seat has an upturned end, there is no lockable compartment included in the specification.

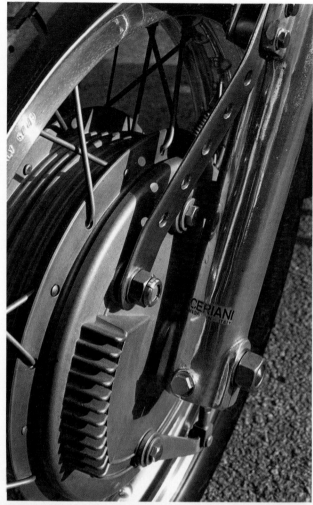

C6

C7

C8

C6. Unmistakably MV, and probably one of the cleanest and best cast of all motorcycle crankcases. The centre section is finned to aid cooling in the "dead" area immediately behind the front wheel.

C7. The twin drum front brake is well ventilated and has a stout torque arm drilled for lightness. Both brakes are of the twin leading shoe type.

C8. The camshaft end covers are of unusual, but attractive, shape. Note the use of chrome plated dome nuts and the take-off for the tachometer drive.

C9

C10

C11

C9 & C10. Side panels on the 750S drum brake model are small in area and are painted red, without any relief. The side panels fitted to the disc brake 750S model are much larger in area and are relieved by a white flash.

C11. Apart from the metal model identification badge, the 750S America side panels can be identified by the lourvres cut in the side, in the vicinity of the air cleaner.

C12. The rear of the petrol tank fitted to the 750S America models provides a more angular appearance and tends to give this model a somewhat different appearance.

C13. This effect is accentuated by the much deeper side panels of the America, which blend in with the lower rear edge of the tank.

C14. Another distinctive feature of the America is the black seat and the lockable stowage compartment immediately to its rear. Despite the curves, this too helps to give the "squared off" look.

C15

C16

C15 & 16. Apart from the model identification on the
fairing and side panels, the larger capacity Monza model
has a white flash on the compartment behind the seat.

Note the spoked alloy wheels and that this example is
fitted with gas-filled shock absorbers.

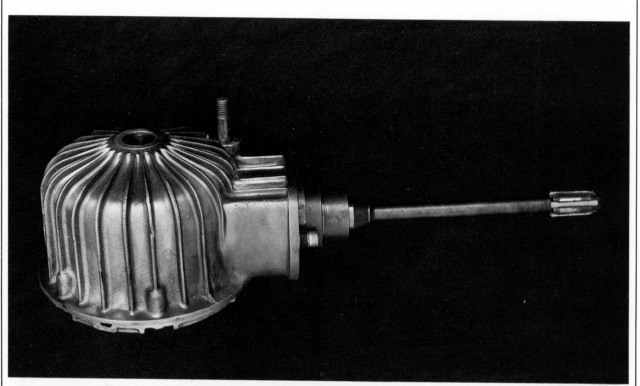

C17

C18

C17. A close-up of the dismantled shaft drive assembly, showing the massive finned bevel cover, the shaft, and the splined coupling on the end.

C18. No caption necessary!